Sarah E. Frazer

I Didn't
Sign Up for This

How to Rest in God's Goodness
When Your Story Shifts

PUBLISHING
BRENTWOOD, TENNESSEE

Published by B&H Publishing Group
Brentwood, Tennessee

Dewey Decimal Classification: 231.5
Subject Heading: MOSES (BIBLICAL LEADER) / PROVIDENCE AND
GOVERNMENT OF GOD / CHRISTIAN LIFE

Cover design by Jennifer Allison.
Illustration by MyStocks/shutterstock.
Author photo by Johnson Photography.

1 2 3 4 5 6 • 27 26 25 24 23

To my husband, Jason. When my story shifts,
so does yours. Thank you for being a part of God's
goodness as we walk this path together.

Acknowledgments

This book's journey has not been a straight line. It was a long, twisty-turn path to find myself here. So many have contributed to this book being out there in the world. First, I want to give a special thanks to my dear editors, Ashley and Clarissa. Their kindness, wisdom, and patience have made this book so much better. Thank you for taking a chance on me. Thank you for taking my story and helping me tell it with grace and humility. Thank you for pointing me to Christ.

I want to thank Compel Training, Proverbs 31 Ministries, and the First 5 team for teaching, guiding, and pushing me to be the best writer I could be. Thank you to my fellow writers who have cheered me on, edited my writing, and invited me into their circles. I feel so honored to know you and be known by you.

Thank you to those friends who spoke words of encouragement throughout the years of rejection. Then when it came to this book, you were there rejoicing with me. Micah, your friendship means more than you will ever know. Rebecca, Anna, Natalie, and Alicia (my Bible study girls), thank you for loving me so deeply all those years we spent opening up God's Word every other Thursday. You walked through most of my story with me.

To my family. Thank you for loving me despite myself. My mom and dad, my in-laws, my sisters, and my brother. Your faithfulness to just be there when we needed help is something I don't take for granted.

A deep and lasting thanks must go to my agent, Keely. Your kindness and dedication to my words has not gone unnoticed. You took a chance on me and walked me through each of the rejections only to help me see this story that was inside of me all this time. Thank you for working so hard on my behalf, and also for being such a kind soul.

To my husband, partner, and best friend, Jason. Thank you for walking every single step with me. Each rejection you allowed me to grieve, then you were there to push me back up. All those times I wanted to give up, you spoke truth and love into my heart. Before the words were written, you and I walked through the grief and unknowns together. Your compassion and wisdom is an anchor for my life. The way you love others and love me has made me a better person. Your unconditional kindness and ability to give so freely of your time and energy for others inspires me.

To my God, thank You for the suffering in my life. Thank You for the darkness and desperation, because in those moments I've found You. In every season You've proven Yourself to be faithful, loving, and good. May I continue to walk further into knowing the depths of Your goodness as my story shifts.

Contents

Let's Not Tell the Truth

There is a picture of me taken almost thirty years ago in a bathing suit behind my parents' house. My dark-brown pigtails are wet and my suit is rainbow—one of those faux two-piece swimsuits where the top and bottom are connected on the sides. I'm standing in the middle of a plastic shallow pool with a huge grin.

I look to be about nine, which means my brother was seven and my sisters were little babies. Life was simple then. I see the girl with the rainbow swimsuit now and think to myself, *You have no idea what your life is going to be. You think it will be simple, straightforward, and predictable.* We all laugh at the idea that life could be neat and tidy. It might be fun to make-believe, but we are not nine years old anymore.

I have a nine-year-old daughter now. She has the passion I remember feeling and she has the bossiness I know I exuded. Looking at that picture, I don't think I would tell that nine-year-old the truth. What I mean is, I don't think I would want to tell a little girl that her plans will most likely be disrupted, rearranged, and disappointed.

I don't think I would go back and tell myself to "watch out" or "be careful." I would let myself make mistakes. I wouldn't even

1

want to go back and warn myself of the twists in the path coming up. Crazy as this might sound, today I *would* want to have my path disrupted. There will be things for this little girl she didn't sign up for, but in those disruptions God revealed more than just my inability to control life. He showed me how even when my plans are rearranged, His plans are not frustrated. God's plan goes forth, no matter what has come before or what lies ahead.

At the time, the assignments I couldn't see coming in my own story didn't feel kind or loving. They felt more like abandonment and disillusionment. They didn't evoke feelings of immense love and appreciation for the Hands of Him who had suddenly changed the course of my life. There was more hurt, feelings of rejection, and confusion than I'd like to admit. Have you experienced disruptions like this—changes in your life that throw you off course and leave you questioning everything, perhaps even your faith?

I didn't sign up for depression after grieving a grandmother nor walking through the brokenness of a difficult adoption. Nor did I sign up to be a missionary for two years to suddenly have the door close in my face. These disruptions have raised hard, even painful questions—about myself, my plans, my trust in God, and even my very faith.

Even so, I would not go back and tell myself the answers. Sometimes questions need to linger because eventually, the good God behind the scenes is going to show up. He always shows up. Often it isn't with answers, but with direction and peace. Maybe if I had to tell my nine-year-old, sixteen-year-old, or twenty-year-old self anything it would be this: *God's sovereign goodness will show up every time.*

If I told my past self about her future children, I would not mention the post-birth depression or how empty and pointless it felt to quit my job to stay at home with a newborn. I would not tell my little girl self that she would have to lose her most-loved grandparent right after giving birth to a second little boy. I would not tell her that the three children she gives birth to will all come in unexpected and heartbreaking ways.

No, I would not warn her about the struggles with anxiety or depression or grief or loneliness or sadness or homesickness because God was present in each situation, and the heartache is sometimes what brings the hidden healing.

I wouldn't even tell her that her dream to be a missionary will come true, but then plans will change and she will find herself struggling to find her footing again.

Dealing with disappointment, disillusionment, and failed plans isn't solved if we "get ready" for the worst-case scenario. It is natural for me to want to think of worst-case scenarios, but this still hasn't kept me from feeling heartbroken.

Our plans will fail. That's a fact of life, and a painful one. Sometimes you might feel like shouting, "I didn't sign up for this!" The shift to understanding why plans failed, and then accepting those changes, finally happened for me when I realized it wasn't about my plans at all. Life isn't about how well I plan, but about God's plan, which reveals His purpose, presence, and promises. My plans will always be shifting and changing, but "God's plans are not written in pencil."

> Forever, O LORD, your word is firmly fixed in the heavens. (Ps. 119:89 ESV)

God's words are true, and they can never be erased. His plans are fixed in heaven. Can this be comforting? Moses certainly thought so.

Exodus 33:9 says Moses would go to a tent outside the camp of Israel and "speak" with God.

> Thus the LORD used to speak to Moses face to face,
> as a man speaks to his friend. (Exod. 33:11 ESV)

Moses was intimately aware of God's Word. In a final prayer to God, he says something all of our hearts need when life hands us disappointment.

> Lord, you have been our dwelling place in all gen-
> erations. (Ps. 90:1 ESV)

More than anything, Moses found a home. What if, even in the middle of the most devastating and unexpected shifts, you found a home in God?

As you journey through this book, you and I are going to walk through the story of Moses, and I hope that you'll come to see the place you belong is found not in a place, but with a person: God— the everlasting God. It is hard to imagine that God can use these rearranged pieces of our lives for His glory, but Moses is going to show us how.

When Moses met God on Mount Sinai, the Lord passed in front of His servant. As God passed over and spoke to Moses, He said,

> "The LORD, the LORD, a God merciful and gracious,
> slow to anger, and abounding in steadfast love and
> faithfulness." (Exod. 34:6 ESV)

Do you want to believe that God is good to you? Trusting that He is good, merciful, and fair takes time. God's goodness becomes more than a big idea or a nice sentiment. As we'll see over the course of this book, focusing on the goodness of God through deep sorrow can become a practical truth to light our way. And God is not only good, but He is sovereign—we need a God who is in control.

What Moses Teaches Us

The other day my daughter made a time line for history class. She printed the pages and taped them together. It was a nice, neat line of events and special memories. But our lives are not straight lines. There are twists and turns and 180-degree pivots.

Maybe we don't need to look back at our lives in order to see how it might have been. We can look back to see where to go next. As we look at our life, even the disappointments, let's look through the lens of someone who has been there too. The Bible is full of men and women who faced setbacks in life. Ruth, Naomi, Joshua, Gideon, Samson, and even the disciples in the New Testament had things in their lives that they didn't sign up for. But perhaps the best person to teach us about disappointment is Moses.

Over the course of his life, Moses faced one blow, disappointment, or disillusionment after another. Yet through it all, Moses was viewed by the writers of Scripture as one of the most humble servants used by God. He is revered as a father of our faith, the prophet who led the greatest rescue plan for the Jewish nation.

This leader and lawgiver lived a long life listening to God. His legacy is summed up in one word: servant. He served God.

> So teach us to number our days, that we may get a
> heart of wisdom. (Ps. 90:12 ESV)

Moses knew that life would be short and frail, and his words are not a warning but an opportunity. We don't need to fear that our "days are numbered." We don't need to worry that unforeseen changes and unexpected detours in our life will ruin what little time we have. We can rest in the fact that each day counts as we move closer to the end. The days we wake up, wash our face, and go do life are precious days. Moses teaches us how to learn wisdom and listen to God, even when we're not sure where we're headed. If we were to trace Moses's life, we would have to make a winding path, but I think Moses would agree that our life is less like a line than a series of steps.

Each step is ordered by the Lord (Ps. 37:23) and they don't always follow a pattern or a path that we can see. Our life is a mixed bag of ups and downs. Good things. Bad things. Unexplained heartache. Disrupted plans. Moses knew what it was like to face rejection, plagues, miracles, floods, death, judgment, weariness, disappointment, and much more. With each turn of events, Moses remained true to God. He continued to lead the people and, most importantly, to listen to God. In the middle of plans being rearranged, Moses remained a servant of God.

A lifetime could be spent studying the life of this great man of God. As we look through Scripture and see a large view of Moses's life, we are going to go through several books from the Old and

New Testaments. We will ask: Who was this servant, friend, companion, and leader of God? What does his story tell us about our own? Might we gain perspective and practical tools to navigate our own challenges and changes?

Moses faced the end of his life, knowing he would never see the fulfilled promise of God's leading the people into the land of Canaan, with these words:

> Satisfy us in the morning with your steadfast love,
> that we may rejoice and be glad all our days. (Ps.
> 90:14 ESV)

Do you feel satisfied with your life today? Do you feel like you are behind, rejected, and alone? Moses felt those things too, but he used those feelings to fuel a faithful life.

Our lives might not be neatly tied up in a bow, but can I propose something to you? What if shifting your perspective actually reveals enough truth to bring happiness back into your life again? What if you could find comfort in God's presence, promises, and purpose for you? What if true rest is just around the corner because of God's goodness in your life today?

Do you want to know why your life matters in God's great plan for redemption? Then join me as we step into Moses's story, and explore our own. My prayer is that over the course of this book, you will come to believe God's promises, and see how devastating setbacks can lead to deeper spiritual growth.

1

Faith Has the First Word

Crammed in the cold lobby, my hands shook with nervous energy. The loud voices and crying babies disappeared when I first saw her face and she entered my arms. Months of waiting ended as I held my little girl against me. Anticipation and excitement turned, instantly, to unexpected worry. Her frame was small, but her lack of muscle tone made her heavy. I could barely keep her from falling out of my arms. She was limp and unresponsive. I sat down on a hard plastic chair in an unfamiliar city in the middle of China. My husband and I exchanged a glance. We knew. Something was not right.

When we adopted our daughter, her special needs turned out to be more severe than we were initially aware. After bringing her back to the hotel room that first day, I called my mother. Through sobs, I told her how things were all wrong. "She is so much worse than we thought. She can't sit up. She can't look at us. She is barely moving. We don't know what this means. She might need lifelong care." *I didn't sign up for this,* I thought, unable to say these final words out loud.

Back home I had three children; ages six, four, and two. I felt overwhelmed thinking about adding a child with developmental delays to our daily life. Those first few days, all of the worst-case scenarios entered my mind. *Will she be able to walk? Will she talk? What about her ability to enter kindergarten? Graduate? Was independent living even on the table?*

It's funny how in those moments of panic, we jump to the conclusion. We try to see as far into the future as we can. I imagined having to care for a child in my old age. I pictured my children arguing over who would take their sister after my husband and I had passed away.

Before this, life made sense. For thirty years, I believed God had a plan and it was good. Isn't that what Romans 8:28 means? Even if bad things happen, it will be okay. All things will be good. Or so I thought. Halfway around the world in a hotel room, I sat on a bed with broken dreams and disillusionment as to what God was doing, unsure of what was happening to my life. God's goodness seemed like a cruel joke.

Have you been here before? Have you experienced a moment or a series of events that knocked you down and suddenly you found yourself saying, "I didn't sign up for this"? I know what that feels like. I know how fearful it can be to find, in an instant, that everything has flipped.

We are often shaped by our parents' lives, so let's take a look at Moses's mother, Jochebed's life, to learn about unexpected challenges and heartache. Before her son had even drawn his first breath, the enemy was planning his demise. With her son's birth, her life was going to be thrust onto an unexpected path.

In Exodus chapter 1, Moses introduces us to his mother and gives us the context in which his story will emerge. He begins with a brief description of how bad it was for the Hebrews. When the small tribe of seventy people initially came from Canaan, the Pharaoh was kind to them. Joseph was the son of Jacob, the leader of the tribe, and Joseph was favored and loved by the king of Egypt. One, maybe two generations later, however, all of the goodness was gone. A new Pharaoh arose who didn't know Joseph. He hated and feared the children of Jacob, the nation that would be Israel. He feared they would overtake his kingdom, so he decided to preemptively attack.

The first blow was to put the Hebrews into slavery. Exodus 1:14 says, "And they made their lives bitter with hard bondage—in mortar, in brick, and in all manner of service in the field. All their service in which they made them serve *was* with rigor (Exod. 1:12).

The Pharaoh continued to be afraid of the Israelites. His next plan was to kill their male babies before they could become men. He instituted a law requiring all boy babies to be put to death.

> Then Pharaoh commanded all his people, "Every son that is born to the Hebrews you shall cast into the Nile, but you shall let every daughter live." (Exod. 1:22 ESV)

Imagine the heartache, fear, and uncertainty each Hebrew woman faced as her rounded belly grew. The Nile River was to consume their baby boys, and all of Egypt would carry out these deathly demands.

Despite the work, service, bitterness, death, and fear, God's people continued to grow. God was going to raise up, among these poor, desolate, and pitiful people, a man who would lead them from slavery to absolute freedom. Ultimately this man would help establish a nation that would bring eternal redemption for even the Egyptians. But let's not get ahead of ourselves. Heartache, confusion, and many story shifts would need to happen to make this come true. For now, let's take a look at Moses's mother, born into slavery, but designed by God to be the one to have faith.

Jochebed's name isn't even mentioned in Exodus 2, but we know it from Exodus 6:20 and Numbers 26:59. We also know that she had already given birth to two other children. Moses's brother and sister were probably born before the murders were ordered. However, the situation surrounding Moses's conception and birth were much more dire. God would use Jochebed in a special way despite the scary situation. Jochebed possessed the kind of faith we want.

> By faith Moses, when he was born, was hidden
> three months by his parents, because they saw he
> was a beautiful child; and they were not afraid of
> the king's command. (Heb. 11:23)

This verse says Moses's mother and father both had faith enough to keep the baby alive. This is the only verse that gives us a glimpse into Moses's parents' belief. They saw he was beautiful. God somehow had whispered to their hearts, "Keep this child alive." We can speculate as to what "he was a beautiful child" means, but in the end it came down to faith. Hebrews says, "they were not afraid of the king's command." Jochebed had no idea how her life would turn out, but she knew murder was wrong and this child deserved to live.

The Nile River was supposed to be a life-giving river. With its waters, the crops grew and the people were fed. For centuries, it had kept people alive. Now, it would take the lives of the Hebrew baby boys. And so Jochebed hid her baby. In an act of faith she nurtured, loved, and cared for Moses for three months after his birth, keeping his existence a secret. When she couldn't hide him any longer, she placed him in a basket in the river and walked away, trusting God with whatever would happen next. This was her act of faith: even if fear was present, she still believed God had a purpose. We can't know why she chose this nor what ultimately she believed would happen. But we know that her faith, according to Hebrews, was not rooted in fear.

When my daughter was placed in my arms, the overwhelming feeling was fear. This was not the little girl everyone had told us about. She wasn't smiling. She wasn't standing up. Her skin beneath the four layers of clothing had turned a yellowish color. I was overwhelmed, afraid, and helpless. In those moments, I didn't need courage to fight my fears—I needed faith. When life shifts and fear rises up, it isn't wrong to fear, but we can withstand the flood of fear with faith.

What does this faith look like, and how can you cultivate it so that it is present when the hard times hit? Let's consider how Jochebed's faith withstood the river of fear.

This woman believed God had a purpose for her and her family. When doubt threatened to flood her heart, she made an ark of faith. With her example, you too can find the faith to stand against the river of disappointment, uncertainty, and rearranged plans. When your story shifts, it doesn't have to shipwreck your faith.

A Hidden Faith

> The woman conceived and bore a son, and when she saw that he was a fine child, she hid him three months. (Exod. 2:2 ESV)

As the midwife handed Jochebed the baby, she didn't know if it would be a boy or girl. Centuries before ultrasounds, she would have spent her pregnancy uncertain of the baby's gender, uncertain of whether the child would live or die. How much easier would things have been if God had given her a girl instead? There wouldn't have been heartache or a choice to make. Now, seeing her son for the first time, she had to decide. Her plans to raise her children and watch them grow up in a bustling, joyful home were disrupted. We also have a choice to make when life suddenly changes. Will we trust God or be consumed by fear?

Moses's parents hid him because they were "not afraid" of the king's rule (Heb. 11:23). Fear did not get the final word—because faith got the first word. Faith in God was where Jochebed placed her hope. She would care for her son, nurse him, and hide him from the enemy. She would keep him a secret.

Sometimes God asks us to have faith that is hidden from others, as Jochebed's was in the time she hid Moses. As the days passed after Moses's birth, she must have spent time alone and hidden away—unseen and alone in ways she couldn't have anticipated.

Instead of celebrating the birth of a new child with family and friends, accepting their support and love, Jochebed had to keep her son's life secret, trusting God with something that no one else could even know about.

Have you ever had a shift in your story that no one else could even know about? Jesus might be asking you to walk through an unexpected time now where you feel hidden and unseen.

I remember one morning years ago, when I was gently rocking a newborn to sleep. My cold coffee sat on the table in front of me and my prayer journal was empty. I was too tired to even write one word. The "to-do" list from the day before remained unchecked. A sigh escaped my mouth. Then God nudged my soul with this truth: Faith is not for when I am refreshed and renewed; faith is needed when I am tired and empty.

A quiet faith is for moments when you can't go on. Faith when no one else is watching is key to getting through life's interruptions.

A Courageous Faith

> The woman conceived and bore a son, and when she saw that he was a fine child, she hid him three months. (Exod. 2:2 ESV)

The second way in which Jochebed's faith withstood a tumultuous time was through her courage. Maybe Jochebed didn't feel courageous, but being brave means acting in spite of fear—not necessarily without fear. In fact, sometimes fear is an unavoidable part of our lives, especially when plans are disrupted.

Where will we go from here?

What will happen to me?

What will happen to this person I love?

How is this going to work out?

These questions reveal your fear, but can also develop your faith muscles too! You can move forward with courage because of faith. Jochebed was assured that God would work in the life of her son. There was purpose even in a small child's life. Her faith allowed her to hope and act in bravery.

A few years ago, I sat at my dining room table with a girl I had been friends with since childhood. That day, though, wasn't to get together to chat and laugh. She had just lost her baby a few months prior. Struggling with words, we finally just cried together.

I asked, "What is the hardest part?"

"Fear," she said. "I fear the future. I fear I might not ever feel normal again. I fear that something terrible could happen to everyone I know. I'm afraid to get pregnant again."

As she gripped her coffee mug, tears ran down her cheeks. My friend bravely got pregnant again a few years later. Can you imagine the fear that plagued her? *Would the baby be healthy? Would this baby be okay?* Despite her sorrow, she chose to get up each day and move forward, courageously trusting God. Having faith that God is who He says He is.

Our life can turn scary in a moment. We get the diagnosis. Our loved one dies suddenly. Doubts about God's goodness and sovereignty flood our minds. But what is true? When we are out in the storm and our boat begins to rock, God is true. Our faith should always be growing in this life, sure, but it doesn't need to qualify as "perfectly strong enough" in hard circumstances, because our faith isn't dependent on us. Our faith rests in God, who is more than strong enough. It's not our faith itself, but the *object of our faith*—God—who we should look to for ultimate power.

Like Jochebed, my friend was "assured" (Heb. 11:1) of what would come. God would carry her through, so she bravely stood up and said, "I choose to believe in God." Rather than allowing life circumstances to ruin her life, she allowed God to redeem it.

God's great redemption plan means we might have to step out and do that very hard task God has placed on our heart. Or maybe it means we simply endure this quiet season of hiddenness with faith and peace. Either way, courageous faith has its foundation in the comfort of God's Word.

We don't know what Jochebed really believed because God's Word hadn't been written yet. Yes, she probably knew the stories about Abraham, Isaac, Jacob, and Joseph. She knew that the God of her fathers had spoken to these four men and had a promise for them. But God hadn't physically shown up for her (yet). Sometimes courageous faith means stepping out or believing in a God who we have yet to see.

Right after coming home with our daughter from China, my mother bought me a wall decoration. It said, "I'm going to practice courage every day." Years later I still have that sign because I need to remember that courageous faith is a daily choice. Jochebed hid her baby daily, knowing that each day his cries risked their entire family. Each day passed with the chance of neighbors or the

Egyptians finding out about this child. Her entire household probably held their breath in fear, but she chose to be brave.

When life interrupts our plans, we remember God's redemption plan is still working—and maybe we use these interruptions to be courageous. Standing firm means we trust in God. My friend, who lost her son, sent her little girl to preschool last year. Fear doesn't have to have the final voice in our hearts. God can give us courage, and we can have brave faith as we walk even the most uncertain path.

A Surrendered Faith

> When she could hide him no longer, she took
> for him a basket made of bulrushes and daubed
> it with bitumen and pitch. She put the child in it
> and placed it among the reeds by the river bank.
> (Exod. 2:3 ESV)

The third aspect of Jochebed's faith that we can look to is perhaps the most difficult: surrender. Though she clearly wanted to keep her son, doing everything to hide and protect him, she knew she had to surrender his unknown future to God.

Pharaoh had commanded that every son born to the Hebrews was to be "cast into the Nile" (Exod. 1:22 ESV). The word *cast* for this verse means to throw, hurl, and fling away. Just like garbage is thrown out, so would be the precious lives of the Hebrew boys. This is where Jochebed's basket comes in.

When Jochebed comes to the river, she doesn't cast away her son. Instead of flinging her child into the river, she intentionally and deliberately yields him to it, placing him in a basket. The basket was prepared ahead of time, carefully constructed with tar and a tight weave. It would not leak or sink. Jochebed prepared a place for Moses to be safe. In a sense, she obeyed the king's edict as she put her son in the river. Instead of throwing him away, she gave him over to God. When we submit to God, we leave the results up to Him.

The word used for Jochebed's *basket* in the original Hebrew means "ark." Her hands carefully prepared this vessel that would save her son's life. The same word is used in Genesis 6–8 to describe the ark that Noah built to save his family from the flood. Both would be an intricate part of God's plan to redeem mankind. An ark, covered in pitch, saved a family in Genesis but also a tiny baby in Exodus.

Do you see how God values even an infant? God values the smallest of us. God values you. Surrendering to God might seem really scary, but the more we know about God the sweeter the surrender.

Jesus is your ark, friend. He is the vessel God uses to give you salvation. We know that salvation only comes through surrender. The beauty of surrender is that we don't have to do anything. Jesus did it all on the cross. A disrupted life allows you another chance to surrender. Will you try to control your situation or will you allow God to work out how to rescue you?

You can surrender to God because His purpose for your life is perfect.

I've learned to hold my plans out to Him. Surrender is sweet. Surrender might feel like giving up at first, but what if surrender is just a giving over? Just as Jochebed gave her plans over to God and placed her son in the river, you can give even the most precious dreams you have over to God.

Sometimes God allows things to happen to us that we would have never chosen for ourselves. It is a hard place to be, especially for me—a planner-control-freak kind of gal. Even though I like to be in control, life rarely goes as planned. Surrendering isn't just letting go, but believing God's plan is better. Trusting that He is still working is a choice. Choose it. The broken dreams, the unheard prayers, and all the times you have questioned whether God is really leading you can bring you to a place of faith. Surrender to His lead because He is trustworthy.

Faith Isn't at the Finish Line

Faith isn't something that takes a hold of us and then we're good. Faith isn't something we choose once—but something we commit to every day. You might find yourself facing pain, uncertainty, and fear, whispering up to heaven the only words that feel honest: "But I didn't sign up for *this*." Know this truth: The enemy wants you defeated. The enemy wants you grieving. Let's rise like Jochebed and choose life and faith. In the moments of his first cry, Moses's life became rearranged. The river would not consume him. His mother's faith stood strong against the waves of doubt.

Faith isn't the finish line because God isn't finished with you or me. If you are holding this book God has plans for your life. Because of His sovereign goodness, God will sometimes allow disruptions to help strengthen your faith. Even in the hardest parts, we can choose to have faith in God's goodness and His sovereignty.

If you find yourself facing a river of uncertainty, may you remember this: the river of fear doesn't have to ruin your faith. Will you experience doubt? Yes. Will you question God's plan? Yes. Will you be afraid? Possibly. These things don't diminish your faith. I used to believe that faith replaced fear. Instead, Jochebed has taught me that faith and fear can stand side by side. Faith can hold fear's hand and tell her, "It will be okay." God is in the middle of our fears with the faith we need to stay afloat.

If we are to see God's hand, faith is required at the very beginning of our journey. We don't want to wait until we've reached the end of this Christian life to have faith. We can start having a settled faith today—not in our abilities or circumstances, but in a faithful God. Remember it isn't our faith that is the key—it is Who we have faith in! The disappointing seasons have the ability to deepen our belief in this truth: God is faithful. Right now, today.

Did this hidden, brave, and surrendered faith permeate Moses's life as well? I think we will see that it did. Moses did not have to include these early details about his mother when he recorded his story, but these particular points lead me to believe Moses drew from his mother's (and father's) faith for the rest of his life. Our hidden places, our courageous acts, and surrendered faith all come from walking through the waters of doubt.

You might not have anything to offer God right now. There might be shattered dreams lying at your feet. The world seems like it is moving on, but you are stuck here picking up pieces of a life you didn't want. If you and I were getting coffee, I would tell you, you don't have to have the answers to have faith. Believe God, even in the deep waters.

Jesus and Moses

In Matthew 14:22–33 we see another man who finds himself in deep water. Peter, an apostle of Jesus, was out on a boat during a storm. Jesus had stayed behind to pray alone up on the mountain. During the night, the disciples crossed the sea. A storm blew them out to the deep part of the water. As they all struggled to gain control, the One who controlled everything walked on water out to their tiny boat.

Peter saw Jesus and asked to join Him on the waves. Jesus said, "Come." Jesus didn't promise to calm the storm, but met Peter in the middle of it. When Peter took his eyes off of the Lord Jesus, it was then he began to sink. The waves crashed, the wind blew, and the cold water pulled Peter down.

Notice that even then, Jesus didn't calm the storm. Jesus didn't even bring Peter into the boat. Instead, Jesus gave Peter His hand. Our Lord and Savior pulled Peter out of the water. Instead of saying, "Why were you afraid?" Jesus said, "Why did you doubt?" You see feeling afraid isn't wrong, it's when our fear overtakes our faith that we sink.

Peter didn't have the ability to walk on water, but he did have a choice. Look at the wind and the waves or look at Christ. We also have a choice when we feel like we are drowning. We can look at everything around us, or can we look toward Christ. God will provide the faith we need.

Just as God saved Moses and Peter from drowning, no matter what kind of fear is flooding your heart today, God will prove Himself faithful in the end. Faith that withstands the storms is a faith that is surrendered, courageous, and often hidden from sight. As we move into Moses's early life, he is going to need this kind of faith. Let's fast-forward a few years in Moses's life to see how God's steadfast, covenant-keeping love gives our faith a foundation.

Prayer

Dear heavenly Father who watched over Moses, be with me today. My life feels like that tiny little basket on the edge of the river. I'm afraid, I want to control my life, and yet I feel unseen and invisible. You made me and You love me, but life feels so confusing right now. Help me trust You, even here. I cannot understand what is going on, but You are still good. I'll admit I don't have the faith I need. Help my unbelief. I need You to grow my faith during this season of interruption. In the midst of even this, You are good. Amen.

Resting in God's Goodness

What has happened in the past month (or year) that made you say, "I didn't sign up for this"? What life circumstances ignite fear in your heart?

_____

_____

What do the following verses tell us about faith?

Romans 10:17

1 Corinthians 2:5

Hebrews 11:1

Circle which one of these you are struggling with the most:

I feel unseen.

I feel afraid.

I feel like my faith is not enough.

We counter unwanted feelings and lies from the enemy with the truth of God's Word. Based on what you circled above, read the corresponding passage. Write what God's Word says in response to your struggle.

I feel unseen. (Ps. 33:18)

I feel so afraid. (Ps. 34:4–5)

God gives us the faith we need. (Rom. 12:3–8)

2

Love, Loss, and Adoption

As we filled out paperwork and I read a mountain of books on the subject of adoption, this phrase kept repeating itself: *Adoption begins with loss.* As I read it, I didn't want to think about the loss. Adoption is really about redemption, right? Romans 8:14–17, Galatians 4:4–5, and John 1:12 use adoption as a picture to show us God's love for us. For me, adoption only represented good things.

But loss is a part of life. What have you lost lately? A job? A friendship? A spouse or loved one? When we lose relationships, health, a loved one, or even a certain future, we realize that life isn't going to ever be the same. We can't go back. When we brought our daughter home from China, our family's daily life shifted in an instant. Loss began to break the foundation of faith we had built.

As we look at Exodus 2:5–10, we are given a glimpse into Moses's childhood. Moses probably felt the sting of loss. He grew up knowing two different worlds. On the one hand he was a son of Pharaoh, but on the other hand he was a Hebrew.

Why did Moses have to be adopted? Why did God's plan for his life include this type of loss? It is easy to skip ahead and look at the end of Moses's story to answer these questions. But let's walk with Moses and see how even this part of Moses's life reflected God's goodness and sovereignty.

When we left Moses in the last chapter, he was a tiny infant in a basket, built by a faith-filled mother. Before we pick up the basket and place it into the arms of a princess, let's remind ourselves that this is not a fairy tale. The princess was not the rescuer of the baby. God had already ordained this woman to be exactly where she was at the exact time the baby cried out in distress.

When we adopted our daughter, we thought we were the ones to "save" her, but true salvation can only come through God. He is the unseen Hero of Moses's story, not the princess. God is the Hero of my daughter's story and He's the Hero of your story too.

Matthew Henry says it perfectly. "God often raises up friends for his people even among their enemies."[1] God used the very household that would destroy, to deliver. The mercy the princess extended to the baby was actually God's mercy on the life of Moses. Moses would learn how to read and write. He would be trained in battle and gain leadership skills as he grew up. Moses not only was saved from dying, he was put in the perfect place to learn how to be a leader.

One of the things we learn in this part of the story is how Moses received his name. Moses was not named by his mother, Jochebed. He wasn't named by an aunt, uncle, or even his sister.

> So she called his name Moses, saying, "Because I
> drew him out of the water." (Exod. 2:10)

Although it was a simple name, with a straight-forward meaning, the princess couldn't know the depths of God's purpose for this child. How could she know that this child would be the mouth-piece and hands and feet of the true Redeemer? God would be the one to deliver His people from the waters of slavery, but Moses would be God's instrument to draw them out. Sometimes God causes the waters to rise, but He also makes a way through.

When our life shifts, it might feel like we are flooded with loss. Everywhere we turn we mourn what was and what could have been and what will never be. Loss after loss floods our hearts, but God draws us out. The princess thought she was the one to deliver the baby from the water. It was in fact the hidden hand of God when she and her maidens walked along the riverside. They "happened" to be there on a normal day doing a normal thing—bathing. It was not a coincidence. As our stories wind down an unknown path it is tempting to think God doesn't know what He is doing. Moses's story reminds us that God orchestrates both the grand moments of life, but also the normal moments.

As soon as she opened the basket, the child cried. In Exodus 2:6 it says the princess "had compassion on him." The phrase *she had compassion on* actually means "to pity." We don't know if her heart was immediately filled with affection. We know she felt sorry for him. She spared him. Did she eventually love him? Maybe, but that isn't told to us. All we know is that God used a normal human emotion to execute His plan. God used the sad cries of a baby to stir a woman's heart.

On the sidelines, we see another girl step forward. Someone else cared for Moses—his sister, Miriam. She had been watching.

> And his sister stood far off, to know what would be
> done to him. (Exod. 2:4)

The poor child needed a nurse. The princess needed help and where did she find it? In the very arms of the baby's mother. When the tiny baby was drawn up out of the water, a courageous slave girl stood up to the privileged princess to offer help. The girl had watched as this tiny baby was placed in the ark of a basket and sent down the river. What would become of him? She had to know. Or maybe she was sent by her parents to watch.

Exodus 2:1–10 reveals two women stepping up in Moses's life. The princess and the sister. They teach us that God uses the people around us when we face the unknown to help us.

When we arrived home with our new daughter, everyone in our church and family knew it would be hard for us. Word spread that she was more disabled than we had thought. Our friends and family circled the wagons. They brought us meals. They prayed for us. They sent cards and clothes. When life was turned upside down, the church was ready to help steady us. What loss are you facing today? How can you reach out and let others help you find your footing? Find the people in your life today who are waiting and willing to comfort you.

God sent Moses's sister and gave her the courage to step forward and offer their mother as a nurse. The princess agreed and even paid the woman to care for her own child (Exod. 2:9). Moses stayed with his biological mother until it was time to be brought to live at the palace.

Seeing God's goodness in the midst of even the most heartbreaking of losses takes time and intentionality. We can look back and see God's goodness in Moses's story, even in deep loss. Can we do the same with our own story?

After we brought our daughter home, my heart began to suspect I would not be able to love her enough to replace what was lost. I'd never had a child flinch away from my touch. I had had three little ones who adored me, and our love for each other was pure and untarnished. For months she never held her hands out to me. My heart broke into a million pieces. I was the one who cared for her throughout the day, but she would pull away from me when I reached for her.

As a mother sometimes you get your heart filled with your children's love. Only my new child at this time couldn't love me back.

I stumbled along until I realized I had all the love I needed in God. Even though I held Bible studies in my home and went to church faithfully for thirty-some years, I was afraid of depending on God's love. Afraid that God's love would run out. When I began to truly believe God's love for me was unending and not based on merit, I was free. I didn't need to earn anyone else's love, including my daughter's.

Moses was both an Egyptian and a Hebrew. Growing up within the walls of two cultures might have felt hard and maybe disorienting at times, but God's love is found even in these moments. Although we are not sure if Moses ever felt it at the time, we can look at this part of Moses's story and see how God's steadfast love and goodness was there even amidst great loss.

What the Enemy Can't Destroy

So Pharaoh commanded all his people, saying, "Every son who is born you shall be cast into the

river, and every daughter you shall save alive." . . .
So she had compassion on him, and said, "This is
one of the Hebrews' children." (Exod. 1:22; 2:6)

Sorrow. Separation. Death. Confusion. Fear. Our God is bigger
and stronger than all of those things. Our God is more holy, more
wise, and filled with more than enough love. The enemy wants to
destroy, but our sovereign God's purpose is beyond the ability to
be ruined. Will we have to suffer loss? Maybe. But God's goodness
means the enemy will not have the final word.

I had dreamed and imagined our daughter would fit the model
of a "normal" child. It was a moment one day, while feeding her
yogurt, when I realized the death of this dream was staring me in
the face. I would not be fixing this. My husband would not be fixing
this. At that moment I felt like God couldn't even fix it. There was
too much to fix. I realized we had a new path . . . and it was one I
didn't sign up for.

The death of a dream brings profound grief. I had never had my
plans unravel to the point of desperation before. It took me months
to recognize and grieve that loss. So if you find yourself looking
at your life and feeling like that tiny infant in the basket, about to
drown in the waters of doubt and fear, start believing this one truth.
Yes, a dream or plan has died. Grieve. Cry. Mourn. Get angry and
ask God why. But remember death is not the end of your story.

God says we have eternal life waiting for us. John 1:12 says we
are "children of God" when we believe in Christ's name. In this
adoption we have life forever promised to us. John 3:16 is not just
a verse for kids at Sunday school. It is the hope and anchor for our
souls when death threatens to unravel us.

"For God so loved the world that He gave His only begotten Son, that whoever believes in Him should not perish but have everlasting life." (John 3:16)

There are things the enemy can destroy. Our plans can be taken from us. There are times when fire and floods consume the plans we make. Other people might step in and steal away our peace and joy. The enemy surely wanted to destroy the baby who would rescue God's people.

Can we see that the enemy doesn't have all authority? God does. And God says death is defeated. Even if your plans fail, those hurts and heartache are not the end of your story. You are still alive. Yes, grief and loss and tears are allowed to be felt. It's okay to keep crying. In the middle of your pain, you cry out to the Father who hears. Even when dreams die, God has not forsaken you.

Who gave the princess compassion? *The God of compassion.*

Who caused her to walk right by the river at that exact moment? *The God who directs our paths.*

Who caused her to see the basket among the reeds? *The God who sees us.*

God says His goodness is greater than any loss we will face. God's goodness is so great it cannot be destroyed; not by you nor by the enemy.

Love Comes with Hands and Feet

Then his sister said to Pharaoh's daughter, "Shall I go and call a nurse for you from the Hebrew women, that she may nurse the child for you?" And Pharaoh's daughter said to her, "Go." (Exod. 2:7–8)

Three women stood up and saved Moses out of the river that day. God used the compassion of one, the bravery of another, and the faith of a third to keep Moses alive, safe, and exactly where he needed to be. These women were different nationalities, different ages, and of different social statuses.

The princess was the only one who would have been able to stand before the Pharaoh and save Moses's life. And she did. The compassion God placed in her heart caused her to be the actual hands and feet of love. We can't assume emotions and feelings in the biblical text, but we can see how God often uses the normal emotions and feelings of women to accomplish His will.

The bravery of Miriam can be seen in her stepping up and speaking out. Could she have remained hidden? Of course. But God stirred her spirit to step out of hiding and ask if the princess needed help. God might be asking us today to be willing to step out and in an act of bravery either ask for help or offer help.

The faith-filled mother who placed her baby in the basket was given a second chance. Her faith was rewarded with more time. No, this wasn't what Jochebed had planned, but let's remember that sometimes God has a bigger plan for us. We need only trust. God is calling us to be compassionate, brave, and faith-filled women who use our emotions to love others. Which woman can you relate to today? Is God giving you courage to stand up and speak the truth? Maybe today you feel compassion and God is urging you to reach out. No matter our status or background God can use each of us.

Healing While Still Hurting

Many years ago, my home church found itself without a pastor. Right about the same time a pastor found himself without a church. While the deacons interviewed other men for the job, this older gentleman was asked to be an interim pastor. He agreed to preach on Sundays until we could find a permanent replacement. He had been pastoring a church not far away but was transitioning to a different ministry.

For a year and a half this pastor preached from God's Word. He opened the Bible and taught our small congregation. We were encouraged and strengthened by God. God used this time to guide us through a time of healing. You see, he had been hurt from his previous pastorship and we had been hurt as a church.

Do you know what God did to heal both the congregation and this pastor during a time of loss? Something miraculous.

When he prepared to leave, after we had found a permanent pastor, this man shared how God had used the months of preaching, and our church people, to heal his heart.

Our church had wrapped our own hurting arms around him, only to find him doing the same. Together we held and healed each other. It was such a special time for our church. Often, I think about what would have happened if that pastor had not come. I believe in all honesty our church would look different today. What an amazing truth: two broken things, coming together, being mended by God.

> Blessed be the God and Father of our Lord Jesus Christ, the Father of mercies and God of all comfort, who comforts us in all our tribulation, that we may be able to comfort those who are in any trouble, with the comfort with which we ourselves are comforted by God. (2 Cor. 1:3–4)

Moses's great loss was made a little less dark because of these three women. They were not perfect. They were just as broken as Moses and they were just as broken as we are. But we have hope that God can use us, even when loss permeates our disrupted plans. How? By loving those around us. We can lift our heads and see how to be the hands and feet of love. We have a unique position to be the hands and feet of love. Our compassion, bravery, and faith can fuel us as we move forward.

Yes, our losses can be redeemed, but they can also help shape the way we help others. Even if our stories contain chapters of loss, we can see those same pages reveal God's love. Moses had the love of a princess, a slave girl, and a mother. There are people who will stand with you and be the hands and feet of Jesus when you face deep loss.

God's goodness sometimes comes with physical help. Do you find yourself struggling to find a footing with the loss you've experienced? You are not without friends. Jesus walks with you, but so does the church. Let the people of God surround you and lift you up. Be willing to open up and ask for help. When it comes, accept it. For in accepting the love of others, you are saying yes to accepting God's goodness for your life.

Adoption Means Love

And the child grew, and she brought him to
Pharaoh's daughter, and he became her son. So
she called his name Moses, saying, "Because I
drew him out of the water." (Exod. 2:10)

Those words, "and he became her son" speak of adoption.
Although adoption comes with loss, we see that because of God's
sovereign goodness adoption is actually an amazing picture of
God's love for us.

We aren't exactly sure what it meant for Moses to be adopted
by Pharaoh's daughter. Some have suspected he would have been
heir to the throne of Egypt. Others say Pharaoh had dozens of
daughters, so the likelihood he would have been king were slim.

What we do know is that adoption meant Moses grew up in
the palace. He had the rights, privileges, and access to the type of
education he would need later.

Adoption would help set the stage for the rest of Moses's life.
Just because loss marks our story, doesn't mean God's plan is
ruined. What if our greatest loss, or greatest disruption, actually set
us in a place to receive the life God had for us all along?

If we were not orphans and desolate because of our sin, God
would have no need to save us. What great mercy we see here!
If we, as fallible humans with sinful hearts can love children who
were not birthed by us, how much deeper, fuller, and steadfast is
the love of the heavenly Father for His very own children whom He
created!?

It is much simpler to blame our disrupted plans on a God who doesn't love us. What if those plans actually point us to the love that has been there all along? God's purpose was greater than Moses could see. Love means God sees the greater, bigger story. Because we trust our loving God, we can see His goodness and love even when we face things we didn't sign up for.

God's Love Isn't Messy

Adoption is messy and complicated. Just because I'm an adoptive mother doesn't mean I understand every single adoptive mother. Nor can I understand those who have been adopted. What I do know, from the Bible, is that God's love for us and adoption into His family is not complicated or messy. God's love is infinite and beyond comparison.

For God, adoption was planned before we were even created. In eternity past, God prepared to adopt us (Eph. 1:4–6). Which means God chose us before we even had a chance to say yes to Him. Why? Adoption reveals the glory of God. When God adopted us, we didn't do anything good. It was all for His glory and our good. There never was and never will be earning His love.

> But when the fullness of the time had come, God sent forth His Son, born of a woman, born under the law, to redeem those who were under the law, that we might receive the adoption as sons. And because you are sons, God has sent forth the Spirit of His Son into your hearts, crying out, "Abba, Father!" (Gal. 4:4–6)

A father to the fatherless, a defender of widows,
Is God in His holy habitation.
God sets the solitary in families;
He brings out those who are bound into
    prosperity;
But the rebellious dwell in a dry land. (Ps. 68:5–6)

God didn't need to react to our sin, God had already prepared the answer. Adoption is not "Plan B." If God has prepared our heavenly future, then God has also prepared our earthly future. We can believe God is already good and the enemy is not strong enough to destroy God's love for us. You might not have signed up for loss, but love can show up anyway.

Jesus and Moses

"For God so loved the world . . ." How do we know this? The rest of John 3:16 says, *". . . that He gave His only begotten Son, that whoever believes in Him should not perish but have everlasting life."* Through the life, death, and resurrection of Jesus Christ we see this redemptive love play out.

> "And I [Christ] have declared to them Your [God's]
> name, and will declare it, that the love with which
> You [God] loved Me [Christ] may be in them [you
> and me], and I [Christ] in them [us]." (John 17:26)

Christ loved us enough to die for us, but the love didn't stop there. The love Christ loves us with not only came from the Father, but is rooted in the Father. If the Father cannot stop loving the Son, then how can we expect the Son to stop loving us?

No matter what loss you face, what waters threaten to drown you, what heartache and grief you carry, God has promised to love you. In His love we find healing. In His love we have confidence. In His love we have a family, a place, and a home. His steadfast love? The one the psalmist speaks about here, this love is for you:

> Give thanks to the LORD, for he is good, for his steadfast love endures forever. (Ps. 136:1 ESV)

In this same love we find acceptance. Just because your life has been turned upside down doesn't mean God has forsaken you. His love is the foundation for our faith but this love is also the basis for this amazing truth from Ephesians 1:6: "To the praise of the glory of His grace, by which He made us accepted in the Beloved."

In the next part of Moses's life we are going to see how God can use rejection in our lives to remind us that we are accepted.

Prayer

Dear Father, who loves me and cares for me, it is hard for me to accept Your love sometimes. I admit. I want to earn it. Intellectually I know I can't purchase Your love with my good works. But in my heart, I am bent on wanting to earn Your love. Destroy this part of me. Get rid of these thoughts today. I pray that the word of truth will be rooted inside my soul and grow a flower of trust. Help me believe and give me the faith to know that Your love for me is more than a river. It is the ocean. In Jesus's name, Amen.

Resting in God's Goodness

What has happened in the last few weeks, months, or years that made you feel like life was just a complete loss? It might have been a series of events, a feeling or emotion that has been growing, or it might have been one thing. Write down at least one or more things you are grieving right now.

What do the following verses tell us about God's love for us? Which of the verses speak to your heart today about God's love for you?

1 John 4:9–11

Romans 8:37–39

Isaiah 54:10

Have you tried to "earn" God's love? So often I think I am one mistake away from losing His love for me. So I focus all of my energy on being a nice person, not sinning, and doing what others expect me to do. What do these verses about love tell us?

Ephesians 2:8

Jeremiah 31:3

Write the name of a person you know who is experiencing loss right now. How can you be the "hands and feet" of God's love for them this week? Circle one of the options on the next page and then do it!

NAME: _____

Send a text.

Make a meal.

Give them a call.

Have coffee together.

Other _____

3

Rejected but Accepted

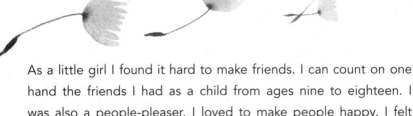

As a little girl I found it hard to make friends. I can count on one hand the friends I had as a child from ages nine to eighteen. I was also a people-pleaser. I loved to make people happy. I felt seen and loved when I knew someone liked me. So when a friend rejected me as a young adult, I didn't know how to feel. Especially since it all happened over some remarks I made to her.

Even though my motives were pure and my words were rooted in truth, I handled the situation incorrectly. In the end she rejected me as her friend. My heart ached because I thought our friendship could survive the disagreement. That break-up shifted my heart in ways I am still unpacking. I thought I would be sharing my future with this friend, but I was wrong. God changed those plans.

When Moses was forty years old, God shifted his life again—in a way that was drastic.

Moses doesn't tell us details about his first forty years of life. Exodus 2:10 tells of his birth, and then Exodus 2:11 jumps to Moses as a forty-year-old man. But in Acts 7:23 we know a little of what happened to Moses during the skipped time.

Life in the courts of Pharaoh influenced Moses in a myriad of ways. The Egyptians were well-educated, and Moses would have studied reading, mathematics, writing, and languages. Moses would have also had training in war. According to biblical scholar James M. Boice, Moses might have even been a commander in an army.[2] In Acts 7:22 it says, "And Moses was learned in all the wisdom of the Egyptians, and was mighty in words and deeds." The Pharaoh probably had many daughters, so Moses was probably not the heir to the throne of Egypt, but certainly Moses would have been allowed to live a life of luxury. But when Moses turned forty, suddenly his path changed.

One day Moses went to see the Hebrews and saw their forced labor. The Bible says he saw an Egyptian beating a Hebrew. Moses defended the Hebrew man by striking the Egyptian dead and hiding the body. Was it a rash act of retaliation or self-defense? The Bible does not comment on this.

The next day Moses left the palace to walk among the Hebrew people again. Suddenly Moses found two Hebrew men arguing. When Moses tried to break it up, they questioned Moses's authority. They said, "Who made you a prince and a judge over us?" (Exod. 2:14). They had seen Moses kill the Egyptian. Moses became scared. When the Pharaoh found out, he tried to kill Moses, so Moses fled Egypt.

According to Acts 7:25, Moses believed God was going to use him to deliver the people. When Moses walked down to visit "his brethren," he was choosing to be associated with poverty, oppression, and suffering. This was a deliberate choice. Although Moses sought to be what God was calling him to be, he didn't go about it properly. Even when we are trying to live out God's purpose for our lives, we will make mistakes.

As we study Moses's choices and actions, we cannot be certain of his feelings. But we can see how God can use disruptions, our sinful choices, or misguided passions to direct us to the place He wants us to be. Moses would later be called "very meek, more than all people who were on the face of the earth" (Num. 12:3 ESV), but at this point in our story, Moses seems anything but meek. We have the ability to look beyond Moses's story and see how God used events like this one, and probably others, to shape Moses into a great leader. Can we have the same vision for our own lives? Maybe a rejection in your life is a way of God moving you to a new place with new people. That might feel a little hard, but rejection doesn't have to define your life. For me, one friendship ended but it opened my heart to other friendships right in front of me.

Some have said that because of this one event Moses "wasted" forty years of his life because he ended up in the desert for forty years. God orchestrated Moses's leaving Egypt perfectly. This was not a waste because God was going to use even this to further His glory and bring goodness to Moses's life. God sometimes uses our choices, good or bad, to direct our path.

The promises we have from God do not change, even when our circumstances shift. The point is not whether Moses was justified in the killing or not. The lesson we have is that God can use any event and the season that follows to reveal His goodness. Rejection of others does not mean we've made mistakes nor does it mean we are innocent. Moses was wrong to kill and the Israelites were wrong to reject Moses as their leader. This part of Moses's story shows us that even if we sin or others sin against us—God's plan goes forth.

Moses probably didn't feel good at that moment. And when other people reject us, it certainly doesn't feel good. We don't have to feel good about where our life is right now. But God can use the rejection of others to show us how much we are accepted by Him.

Rejection doesn't mean God isn't happy with us. It doesn't mean God has left us. Rejection might mean God has some lessons for us, and often those lessons involve learning about who He is.

Independence Isn't Godly

For he [Moses] supposed that his brethren would have understood that God would deliver them by his hand. (Acts 7:25)

Those first few months as a young mother I thought I should have my life together. Okay, even after fourteen years of motherhood I still think I should have it all together. In fact, I don't think I should "look" like I have all of my little ducks in a row—they really should be in a row. I have this internal pressure to make sure my life is organized, planned, and flowing perfectly. Over the years, when my story shifted again and again, God reminded me that I don't have to have it all under control. Being a dutiful wife, mother, friend, sister, and daughter is overwhelming.

I can't do it. Neither can you.

Growing up, I watched all of those old sitcoms and movies that taught that girls can do anything. *Women, don't let men overshadow you. Girls, you can be and do anything. All you need is independence. The right type of woman is the one who is in control and doesn't rely on anyone else.*

Biblically this is not correct. We are inadequate, unprepared, and ill-equipped on our own. We need God. Sometimes God allows us to face rejection and failure in order to teach us this truth. My plans to be a strong, independent woman are often crushed because I have over and over again faced situations which I couldn't overcome.

I was thirty-seven weeks into my first pregnancy. While visiting my OBGYN, I saw my blood pressure was higher than the previous week. My feet ached from the swelling. We sat in that cold waiting room with my big belly making it hard for me to breathe.

After entering the room in a rush, the physician's assistant sat down. I had been expecting the doctor. She quickly said, "I think you're going to have your baby today. The doctor will be in to talk to you about it." Then she left the room less than five minutes later disinterested in answering our questions. Jason sat in the chair, and I sat with my legs dangling off the examination table. We stared at each other with wide eyes.

We waited for the doctor. She came in with a sparkle in her eyes. Her voice bubbled with excitement, "Go home and pack your hospital bag! We are going to induce you tonight. Your blood pressure and tests show that you are probably developing pre-eclampsia. Your baby is coming today!"

I was induced, and in the end gave birth via C-section. It was the complete opposite of my birth plan. God had a lot to teach me about dependence and control. It was during this time God led me to John 15:5 which says, "I am the vine, you are the branches. He who abides in Me, and I in him, bears much fruit; for without Me you can do nothing." See that last word? It says nothing. We cannot do anything without Jesus. Andrew Murray wrote a wonderful book on Jesus called *The True Vine*. In it he sums up the idea of abiding here:

> Abiding in the Vine then comes to be nothing more or less than the restful surrender of the soul to let Christ have all and work all.[3]

One of the things I had to surrender was my independence. God used Moses in a mighty way, and God can use us in a mighty way—but God doesn't need us to be strong and independent. In fact, He needs us to be the opposite. As we will see throughout "the whole story of Moses," it isn't about Moses at all. God will use Moses, but God doesn't need Moses. We can have confidence that working for God and serving Him is rooted in abiding in Him. We might have been rejected but God accepts us . . . in all of our weakness.

In Exodus 2:11–13 Moses was moved with compassion at the injustice and wickedness of the Egyptians toward God's people.

It wasn't wrong for Moses to want justice. It became wrong when he tried to accomplish his desires, whether from God or not, on his own. Moses would need God's power.

Living a faithful Christian life isn't found in my own strength. Only through dependence do we discover God's purpose for our life. If you are struggling today to determine how God can use this life of disruption, depend on God. One of the secrets of God's sovereign goodness is coming to a place where we say, "help me." We are accepted because we are dependent on God.

The Way to God Is Found in the Heart

. . . esteeming the reproach of Christ greater riches than the treasures in Egypt; for he looked to the reward. (Heb. 11:26)

After surrendering to God, relinquishing my control, I struggled with understanding what God's purpose was for my life. How could I feel accepted when I kept failing? I knew He wanted me to be a mom. But what else? I began taking online classes, but that was overwhelming. I started writing on a blog, but God gave me another little boy two years after the first. Suddenly I was up all night with a newborn and instead of being able to sleep in the mornings, my toddler was up at the crack of dawn. God was still teaching me about dependence.

All through the Bible we see God is not concerned with the outward appearance, but with what is inside a person. What we believe about God, what we believe about ourselves, and how we are growing spiritually is honestly more important than what we do on the outside.

Do you want to walk in the ways of God? Moses did, but what Moses learned is that we cannot walk in the ways of God, accomplishing God's purpose for our lives, if we are doing it in our own strength, or our own way. We need to walk the path God has laid out for us—and often He will give us things that bring us back to Him for help. Something I didn't plan on as a new mother was this feeling of weakness. It turns out after both boys were born I struggled deeply with depression.

How could I find God's goodness when I was struggling with deep, dark postpartum depression? Where was all this fruit I was supposed to have because I was relying on God? I didn't sign up for this type of Christian life way back when I was sixteen and I surrendered my plans to God.

God had a glorious, amazing purpose for Moses's life. God's purpose for our life isn't determined by us. Nor will His purpose for our lives take a straight line. The path God has for us might be twisted. Think of others in the Bible: Abraham, Judah, Joseph, Ruth, and the apostles. Just because our path is interrupted, doesn't mean God's purpose is interrupted. God's purpose for Moses, in spite of everything in Exodus 2, moved forward.

John 15:16 says,

> "You did not choose Me, but I chose you and appointed you that you should go and bear fruit, and that your fruit should remain, that whatever you ask the Father in My name He may give you."

If you are a child of God, God has chosen you to bear fruit. God's way always includes fruit. Some we see now, but often we don't see the fruit until later, if at all. As we look at our path as distorted and sometimes shady, let's not get tempted into thinking God has left us. We can learn to embrace this season, knowing God's way and God's purpose has not been destroyed by either our own mistakes or others.

God Is Bigger Than Our Loneliness

> But Moses fled from the face of Pharaoh and dwelt
> in the land of Midian; and he sat down by a well.
> (Exod. 2:15)

The words *face of Pharaoh* is a phrase that means the "presence of Pharaoh." Moses ran to the land of Midian.

Starting over is never fun nor does God allow this pain into our hearts haphazardly. It often leads to suffering, and a season of loneliness might await us after being pushed aside.

God's way doesn't always lead us to where we think we want to go. God leads us to where we can be like Christ. After my friend's rejection, I sought the Lord in the pages of the Bible. Each day I asked God to fulfill that need for me. God became my friend.

Today, as I write this, I'm also facing a season with very little friendship. My days are lonely, but looking back at how God showed up for me in that season over ten years ago reminds me that God will show up for me now. Reminding ourselves of God's promises fulfilled keeps hope alive that God will keep the promises that have yet to be seen.

When all we have is God, He is all we need. During that time ten years ago, I prayed, I studied, but I also spent a lot of time asking God to give me another friend. Just because we acknowledge God has led us here, doesn't mean we have to stop searching for His will for our lives. If rejection by others is a part of your story, something you didn't sign up for, just know God does not want you to live alone. God doesn't bring us to this hard place to fend for ourselves. We were made for community. And sometimes God provides it in unexpected ways.

> But Moses fled . . . and dwelt in the land of Midian;
> and he sat down by a well. (Exod. 2:15)

God's path for Moses led him to a well. There will be people and situations where God will remind us that He is enough and we will have what we need. They will be like finding a well in a desert. The nourishment we need might be just around the corner.

As we continue Moses's story in the next chapter, the Midianites accepted and embraced Moses in his exile. We can also find acceptance. After that friendship ended, I struggled to make friends again. It takes me a long time to feel as if I can open up. When I do, I spend the next weeks second-guessing everything I said to that person. But God is still faithful to provide a friend when I need one. Even now, as I face a lonely season, God is daily reminding me that He is the friend who sticks closer than a brother. God always provides Himself as a comfort during those seasons.

Today I want to remind you of something I still need to hear. Rejection is not the end. It will disrupt and displace you, but the feelings of sorrow, rejection, and failure are not the end. God uses these seasons and dare I even say leads us to these seasons, on purpose. Often it is to reveal truths about Himself we would not otherwise know. One of the truths He wants us to know is that His promises are still true.

Jesus and Moses

The most beautiful thing about rejection is we are not alone in facing it. Everyone might leave you. Moses left Egypt alone.

No family. No friends. And yet he didn't travel alone for very long. Friend, if you have been traveling down this disrupted path alone, facing the rejection and loneliness that comes from broken dreams, it is time to find a well.

Jesus knows exactly the path you walk.

One day He sat beside a well to wait for a woman who was rejected. In John 4 we read how the woman at the well came alone, but Jesus met her there. How could He speak to her deep need? Because our Lord and Savior walked this earth for thirty-three years. He spent time alone. He was misunderstood, rejected, and even at times His own family didn't believe Him. In John 17, Jesus tells us that rejection is a part of being a Christian. With that rejection comes acceptance. You see, Christ might have been rejected, but it was all for the purpose that we would be accepted.

> He is despised and rejected by men,
> A Man of sorrows and acquainted with grief.
> And we hid, as it were, our faces from Him;
> He was despised, and we did not esteem Him. . . .
> But He was wounded for our transgressions,
> He was bruised for our iniquities;
> The chastisement for our peace was upon Him,
> And by His stripes we are healed. (Isa. 53:3, 5)

Even if other people reject us, we can hold fast to God's goodness because it holds fast to us. God's love for us will keep, guard, and lead us (see Ps. 121). Christ was exiled so you could be accepted. Your lonely season will not last forever. God is still leading and while He leads, He is loving you.

Christ was rejected. Not because He sinned but because in rejection Christ was able to redeem us all. Even if others turn away from us or dismiss us, we can have faith, rooted in love, to keep going. Although we might be left out, God has a place for us just like God made a place for Moses among the Midianites.

Living in God's sovereign goodness is where we find divine acceptance, even if rejection is a part of our story. That place of rejection might lead you and me to a season of loneliness, but our lonely seasons can bear much fruit. Moses walked away from Egypt to live a life in the desert. What he might have thought would be a season of emptiness, actually proved to be the very thing to grow him into the leader God would eventually use.

Prayer

Dear heavenly Father, as I move forward today, I acknowledge that sometimes I feel rejected, alone, and filled with weariness. I rejoice that You understand me. You suffered rejection. You suffered on the cross. You endured the cross and rejection of men so that I may come to the Father and know the sovereign goodness of acceptance. Lord, You have not rejected me, but have called me to come to You. God, You are still good, even when I face rejection and loneliness because You are still leading me. Create in me a heart that knows and remembers I am accepted by You today. In Jesus's name, Amen.

Resting in the Goodness of God

Think of a time when you felt rejected. Maybe a person's face is in your mind right now. Maybe a work situation has you remembering those feelings of hurt and sadness. Circle the words that best describe how you felt during that time:

Lonely.

Misunderstood.

Alone.

Failure.

Sinful.

Lost.

Weary.

Apart.

Read these verses about God's acceptance of us.

Ezekiel 36:26–28

1 Peter 2:9

Romans 11:15

During a season where you feel rejected, it is important that you remember that though someone might have turned their back on you, not everyone feels the same. Not only do you have a God who loves and accepts you, but there are people in your life who love you. Write down at least three people who you know love you.

_____

_____

_____

Christ endured many types of rejection during His lifetime. According to Hebrews 4:15, Christ knows all about how we feel when we face rejection. How does knowing that Jesus understands our rejection help you find comfort today?

_____

_____

_____

4

Walking an Unexpected Journey

The bathroom floor was cold. As I sat there in my pj's in the dark, the tears streamed down my face. I was at the bottom of the pit. On the floor of the bathroom, crying, I was desperate. It was during my third trimester with my third child. Depression was a word I whispered to my husband as he crouched down to hold my hand while I sobbed. This wasn't supposed to be part of my story. Why was I feeling this way?

Gently, he pulled me up off the floor. I felt the heavy weight of the child I was carrying. We turned on the light because even artificial light is better than complete darkness. I sobbed and asked why. He didn't say much or offer an answer. There was no answer. We both finally fell asleep exhausted. The bottom of the pit does not provide any answers.

On the outside, my life looked good and right and true. I went to church, prayed, and held a Bible study in my home. The truth was I was struggling deeply with anxiety and depression each night with no hope in sight. It felt like it was for no reason.

I remember telling my husband one night, "If I only had a *reason* to feel this way, it would make it easier." It was the first time in my life I really felt as if God had abandoned me. I knew God cared and loved me because the Bible said so. During the day I would pour into my heart the truth from God's Word, but it all felt empty because the sun would set, and night was the worst. The dark feelings would bubble up and I would cry every night.

This wasn't the first time I had felt this way. Throughout my high school and college years I would react to stress by turning inward and feeling depressed. I am a planner, control-loving, and get-things-done kind of woman. I don't have time for depression. Whenever those feelings would come during high school or college, I would push them aside. I never dealt with them and stuffing it way down deep inside my heart seemed like the best solution.

Until I couldn't anymore. That night on the bathroom floor I realized I had stuffed too much. Nothing else would fit. The feelings were stuffed so tight the suitcase of my heart was ripping open, breaking the zipper. After those weeks of crying each night, my depressed feelings would not be stuffed back in. The case was broken, and those emotions were going to have to be dealt with now. Help came in the form of talking to a counselor and taking medication.

I'd like to say everything was fixed but that isn't true. Instead, God put me on a different path. Today, as I write this, I still struggle with depression. Anxiety has been added to the mix in recent years. It has been almost ten years since that night on the bathroom floor and God has yet to take this away from me completely. But I've found help in a variety of ways, and I don't always feel like the darkness is drowning me.

Depression is like a dark cloud. Hanging over me and following me. It doesn't always feel horrible, but every so often I feel the darkness seeping into my heart. I'll spend a few days fighting the feelings. Then I'll feel better, but my depression has never been cured. Depression was something I really didn't sign up for. Who would sign up for sadness? I wanted to move on with my life, but not dealing with depression made me feel stuck in this place I didn't want to be.

You might be walking through a season of life you didn't sign up for. Does today feel empty and maybe a little disorienting? What about loneliness? I felt so alone when I was battling depression. If you don't feel that way today, you've probably walked through periods like this in your life at some point.

If you find yourself all alone—physically, emotionally, or even spiritually—God's promises don't seem to apply to you. Have you ever asked your heart, "Is God even listening?" You might feel unseen or lonely. You might want to just move and do the work you think God wants for your life. The beautiful thing about walking an unexpected path, is whether we put ourselves there or circumstances out of our control put us there, God is still there.

When we think about Moses, we like to focus on the highlight reel. The burning bush! The ten plagues! The crossing of the Red Sea! Don't worry, there are lessons about his life in those moments, but there is a lesson here. In the time God was preparing Moses as he lived a nomadic lifestyle with the Midianites, God didn't leave Moses even for a second.

Moses sums up the next forty years of his life in just seven verses. The first forty years included life in Egypt and growing up in the courts of Pharaoh. The last forty years will include miraculous moments of God's amazing power, but today we are reading about forty years of quietness. Forty years of Moses faithfully being a shepherd, husband, and father. It would be easy to skip this part of his life, but let's not jump ahead. There are lessons here, as we look at Moses's life with the Midianites.

What Moses thought was the death of a dream, God was actually going to use for His glory and Moses's good. Moses had to say goodbye to family, friends, and all he knew. I suspect you know how that feels. I do. I've had dreams, plans, and wishes for my own life. I've envisioned things for my family only to have the door closed and the dreams die. A shift in our story sometimes means we say goodbye to people or circumstances we have enjoyed and loved.

It says in Exodus 2:15–22 that Moses found himself in Midian. This was an area south of Canaan. The people came from the lineage of Abraham. After Sarah died, Abraham took another wife and she gave birth to six sons (Gen. 25:1; 1 Chron. 1:32). One of those sons was Midian. Although the Israelites as a nation would meet more Midianites on their way to the Promised Land, those encounters would not be positive (Num. 22 and 31). Moses's encounter in Exodus 2 would be different.

Moses sits down by a community well. The God who shifts our story isn't only working in our own lives. He also orchestrates who will meet us. God planned it so that a group of seven sisters arrived at the well while Moses was there. It was common for travelers to find a well and seek lodging during those times. The well served as a hub for people.

At the same time some shepherds came and drove the women away. Moses then rises up (Exod. 2:17) to defend the women. Once again Moses stands up when he sees injustice.

After returning home, the girls tell their father all that had happened at the well.

> And they said, "An Egyptian delivered us from the
> hand of the shepherds, and he also drew water for
> us and watered the flock." (Exod. 2:19)

Moses's rescue stirred their father. Scholars have long argued whether he was a priest of an unknown or Midianite god or the priest of the one true God, or a priest of many gods. It isn't clear, but from various passages and cross references, we can say it is a possibility he believed in Moses's God.

God uses even strangers and foreigners to remind us that we are not alone. In Exodus 2:21 this man gives his daughter Zipporah to Moses as a wife, further welcoming Moses into his family. The Bible says Moses "was content to live with the man." Even though Moses left everything he knew, he found contentment walking this new path.

When we find ourselves on a different journey than we had expected, discontentment is right there as a willing companion. Bitterness is easy and joy is hard to find.

Our family moved to Honduras in January of 2020, but because of COVID, we were limited as to what we could do. In 2021 we were able to finally host our first surgical teams. Everyone on our mission team was working hard translating, cooking, serving, and seeing patients. Do you want to know what I was doing? Nothing. That's what it felt like.

I was busy homeschooling my children and babysitting for a local nurse when the seeds of discontentment began to grow in my heart. I cried at the end of that week because my life felt completely and utterly useless. I couldn't translate because my Spanish was not good enough. I couldn't help medically because I'm not a nurse nor could I help with meals. The enemy used that time to sow dissatisfaction, which led to weariness and sorrow.

God might lead us to a place that feels empty, but God does not lead us to feelings of bitterness. God always has a purpose. Unhappiness is from the enemy, not God.

Exodus 2:21 says Moses "was content to live." As we study these aspects of Moses's life in the desert, we are going to see life might not feel good, but God was and is already good. God's goodness offers complete contentment when we seek Him. Moses found two things in the desert, both of which reveal a character shift in Moses.

Before Moses left Egypt he was physically in the perfect place where God could use him. He was a prince of Egypt and had the ear of the king. Moses was intelligent, well read, wealthy, and powerful. He had military training and had been taught how to be the best leader. Moses was young, only forty years old, unmarried, and in a perfect position to lead God's people.

Moses must have needed something else because God led him to living with the Midianites for a reason. In that time of quiet living, on this new path, Moses found community, contentment, and character.

Community

> He gave Moses his daughter Zipporah [for a wife].
> She gave birth to a son, and he [Moses] called
> his name Gershom, for he said, "I have been a
> sojourner in a foreign land." (Exod. 2:21–22 ESV)

Moses surely felt like an outsider and alone, but God was doing a work in his heart. Moses had two sons while living in the desert (Exod. 2:22; 18:4 ESV). One of the things I love about biblical names is that there is so much meaning behind each one. The first son of Moses was named "Gershom," which means "sojourner, a temporary dweller, or new-comer." Another meaning is "alien, stranger, or foreigner." Moses walked on this new path without a home or family at first.

God didn't leave Moses empty, but provided for Moses a deeper sense of community. Moses found a sense of home and family there among the Midianites. We know this because of the name of his second son. It says he was named Eliezer. His name means "Help of my God."

> And the name of the other [was] Eliezer (for he said,
> "The God of my father was my help, and delivered
> me from the sword of Pharaoh"). (Exod. 18:4 ESV)

What did this community and family bring to Moses? A sense of dependence. Moses finally recognized that God would help him be the leader he knew he was to be.

On these new paths we find ourselves, walking in the unknown, there are people waiting and willing to step into our lives and love us. It might be hard to see, but who can you reach out to today and simply ask for prayer?

No community is perfect. Sometimes God brings people in our lives who are like family. We have definitely experienced that as missionaries living so far from our biological family. You might not have any biological family near or close to you—emotionally or physically. God can provide enough family to us so that we can see His goodness even when our path is unexpected.

Contentment

> Then Moses was content to live with the man, and
> he gave Zipporah his daughter to Moses. (Exod.
> 2:21)

Something else Moses found with the Midianites was contentment. It would have been easy for Moses to turn his back on God after starting over. Instead, Moses embraced life, content to be a shepherd for the rest of his life.

During my life I have walked through multiple seasons where I was discontent. I didn't like my house. Or I hated my job. There was a time when I had my two little boys under foot and felt like life was on an endless cycle of diapers.

During those seasons where we find ourselves living very ordinary lives, we can learn how to be content. Whether you face the daily ins and outs of a life you didn't sign up for, or one that you did, but now it's hard, Moses can show us the value of living the glorious ordinary. In his devotional, *My Utmost for His Highest*, Oswald Chambers wrote one of my favorite quotes:

> Walking on water is easy to someone with impulsive boldness, but walking on dry land as a disciple of Jesus Christ is something altogether different. Peter walked on the water to go to Jesus, but he "followed Him at a distance" on dry land (Mark 14:54). We do not need the grace of God to withstand crises—human nature and pride are sufficient for us to face the stress and strain magnificently. But it does require the supernatural grace of God to live twenty-four hours of every day as a saint, going through drudgery, and living an ordinary, unnoticed, and ignored existence as a disciple of Jesus. It is ingrained in us that we have to do exceptional things for God—but we do not. We have to be exceptional in the ordinary things of life, and holy on the ordinary streets, among ordinary people—and this is not learned in five minutes.[4]

Faith has confidence in the invisible truth that God is present, in both the grand moments and the ordinary moments. Moses eventually did see a glimpse of God on the mountain, but that isn't what kept Moses going. Moses was faithful to God because he had learned how to be faithful in the ordinary times.

Contentment requires endurance. Contentment is not a one-time act. We do not find contentment in God once, then go about our lives. Contentment is a way of life. We know Moses found this at least at the end of his life in his prayer to God in Psalm 90. He writes:

> Oh, satisfy us early with Your mercy,
> That we may rejoice and be glad all our days! (v. 14)

Character

> Now the man Moses was very humble, more than all men who were on the face of the earth. (Num. 12:3)

In this verse we see that something happened to Moses from the time he left Egypt at the age of forty and the time he was leading the people of God through the wilderness.

Sometimes God lets our path be interrupted because we need to develop some more Christlikeness. What if the path you find yourself on right now is actually God growing you? The time of struggle, loneliness, emptiness, and rejection isn't fun. Those times when life is ordinary and boring don't bring excitement to our hearts. These are not the moments we share on social media. In the quiet, sometimes dark seasons, God is still working.

One day my daughter took an avocado seed from an avocado we had eaten. She laid it out on a paper towel to dry, then put it in a pot with some dirt. Next, she sat it outside on our front porch in Honduras. I'd pass that little pot of dirt every day and sigh. I told her it might not grow. A few months later a little sprout sprung up. One day there was a full-fledged plant. While I passed by, under the soil, something was growing. In the dark something was breaking apart and making something new.

As I was sweeping the porch one day, I noticed the seed was sticking out of the dirt. If you've ever seen an avocado seed, you know they are pretty big. You could see the part of the seed that had been broken. The green stem was coming from the broken piece. I tucked the little seed back down into the dirt. Why? Because seeds need to grow in the dark. Moses saw the invisible God while living with the Midianites. He believed in what he couldn't see. We don't know how or in what way Moses changed inwardly. Yet, we see the character growth because in the next chapter the rash, young man who killed the Egyptian is going to humbly bow before a burning bush and hesitate to step into the spotlight again.

Years ago, when I was deep in the depths of depression, I felt unseen, unloved, and extremely alone. But that was a time of growth for me. I felt like a broken seed. Useless. Unable to really move forward with my life. Waiting. What can grow in the dark? What can grow in a season that isn't flashy, or shiny, or even public?

Moses grew into the man he was supposed to be while hidden away, not on stage. Platforms are all people talk about when it comes to life these days. Only those squares and captions and sentences online are not real life. Life is lived even when the social media is quiet. Character grows while no one watches.

What can grow in the dark? Let me tell you what God can show us during seasons of hiddenness. We can gain a better picture of who we are and who God is. What God wants to teach you in this season of life is not the same thing He taught Moses. It isn't necessarily what God taught me during my season of depression. God revealed community and contentment to Moses, but for me God showed me some anger issues and controlling tendencies I needed to deal with during that time. I also saw God's ability to sit with me in the darkness and not judge me. He became a light to me and His Word was my precious treasure moving forward.

One thing I know for sure is this—you will see God's goodness. Do we always want or choose this unexpected path? No, but instead of crossing our arms, sitting down, and waiting for God to move us into the next season, let's embrace this life we are called to right now.

The thing is, Moses didn't sit idly by for forty years. He worked. He served. In Exodus 3:1 it says Moses was tending the sheep of his father-in-law. Let's live our lives, right now, working and serving a good and sovereign God who sees us, even in the dark.

Do you feel ignored, unnoticed, and ordinary today? You aren't alone. Moses lived forty years like that. To be exceptional in the ordinary and to see the glorious in the ordinary, we need to have God's supernatural grace.

Jesus and Moses

Jesus Christ also spent time in the desert. Right before He began His earthly ministry, Jesus spent forty days in the wilderness. Many churches celebrate the season of Lent to reflect on and repent of their sin right before Easter. They do so to remember Jesus's time in the desert (Matt. 4:1–11).

Jesus did not go into the desert on a whim; the Holy Spirit led Him there. God also led Moses to the desert. Jesus and Moses spent a period of forty in a desert. Many scholars agree that forty signifies a time of testing and temptation. The prophet Elijah spent forty days in the desert, being fed by ravens while a king and queen sought his life (1 Kings 19:7–9). All three kings, Saul, David, and Solomon, reigned for forty years. Noah, in Genesis 6–9, endured forty days of constant rain while living in the ark.

Forty is also a number that represents a generation. What if our entire life is wrapped up in desert living? What if we get to the end of our life and we never have a certain prayer answered? What if a life of solitude was what God asks of us? What if this thing you have prayed and prayed to be taken away, never is?

Can we continue living in this desert? Friend, you and I might not see why we must live here, but we can see the Who in our season of hardship. We can believe God is still here when we see that the desert does not take away God's love, acceptance, plan, or goodness. In fact, God has lessons for us. Maybe that lesson is first to see how big and awesome our God truly is? And how very near and close to us He is. First Kings 19:11–12 recounts the story of Elijah's vision of God.

> Then He [God] said, "Go out, and stand on the mountain before the LORD." And behold, the LORD passed by, and a great and strong wind tore into the mountains and broke the rocks in pieces before the LORD, but the LORD was not in the wind; and after the wind an earthquake, but the LORD was not in the earthquake; and after the earthquake a fire, but the LORD was not in the fire; and after the fire a still small voice.

Where was God? In the smallness. God was not in the great strong wind or earthquake. God was in the hidden places. Is God in charge of the big things? Yes, but God is right here as well, in your everyday ordinariness. God might lead us on an unexpected path, but God does not leave us in the dark. God was with Moses, Jesus, and God is with us.

As we will see in the next chapter, God is not finished stepping into Moses's life with unexpected turns. The burning bush was more than a shift in Moses's story and more than a command to step up and lead. The burning bush is going to show Moses, and us, the personal and powerful nature of this great God we follow.

Prayer

Dear heavenly Father, my circumstances are sometimes hard to deal with. I didn't ask to be in this season of loneliness and isolation. O God, I ask that You remind me of the truth that You are my family, and You will provide the faith I need. I understand that sometimes living in the desert is where You have led me, but let me also see that You have not led me here to leave me. God, You are still good, even in the desert. Amen.

 Resting in God's Goodness

During my season of depression, I felt as if I was not moving forward in my life, especially in my Christian walk. I felt like I was hanging on by a thread and barely surviving. List some words that describe how someone might feel when life feels stuck.

_____

_____

_____

Those ordinary days of caring for my children, making meals, cleaning my house, and simply serving my family are not glamorous. But I've seen how God used that time to teach me about faithfulness.

What might God be teaching you in your season right now? What area would you like to see changed in your life today? Could it be that God is working on your character rather than your circumstances?

_____

_____

_____

5

An All-Consuming Fire

March 2020. This will be remembered in history as the date when the world shut down. When a virus made the world stop moving. Everyone can recall where they were when the virus brought every country to its knees. We can all remember those days and moments after it was decided that no one was allowed to leave their home or travel. In March 2020 my family was living in Honduras.

Do you remember pre-COVID when masks, hand sanitizer, Lysol, and the threat of a virus didn't enter your daily thoughts? Prior to COVID a lot of us had experienced interrupted plans or circumstances out of our control. The unique and special thing about this virus was that the impact was felt worldwide. In Honduras, we were on lockdown and 8:00 p.m. curfews were put into effect for four to six months. In the United States masks became a big debate politically, socially, and even among churches.

Every two weeks I remember we had to stand in line for two hours to be allowed to enter the grocery store. When I say, "we," I actually mean my husband. Only one person per family could go on their designated day. You had twenty minutes to shop and then leave. This was the rule for about three months. I remember his first trip back from the store. I was excited to have butter for the first time in weeks!

My husband and I got creative with how we would find other groceries between our two-week trips. Not only were we navigating a new, foreign country, with little knowledge of Spanish, we had to figure out how to do it in a worldwide pandemic. This was not how we envisioned our first year on the mission field. Our plan for him to facilitate surgical teams was postponed. We didn't know the future, but we knew we were suddenly on a totally different path.

For every one of us, God stepped in and rearranged our plans. That year my family experienced a time of isolation, loneliness, and separation. I'm sure you can relate. Others endured job loss, financial threats, and health concerns. Some people even lost loved ones and their own health to this dreadful disease. Even today, a few years later, we still feel the aftershocks of that COVID year. We are all still trying to figure out this new world.

Because we moved to Honduras in January 2020, right around the time of COVID, we have a hard time separating the two events. My children would often say, "I want to go back to West Virginia where they don't wear masks."

Since then, our family has been displaced again. After serving for two and a half years, our first term as missionaries came to an end. We now live back in the States. My life is busy with activities and children and homeschooling, but there are still days I feel so defeated. Moving to Honduras and then leaving has changed the course of my life in such a way that there is no "going back." I am now on a path, and sometimes I whisper to God, "I didn't sign up for this . . ."

God disrupted everyone's plans with COVID. More than that, as we travel through this new world of masks, protocols, and social distancing, our hearts are weary to return to what life was like before 2020. But we can't return. There will be no going back to pre-COVID. What happens when God shifts our lives so much that there is no going back to life "before" the event?

After looking at Moses's experience with God at the burning bush, maybe we can see how a great disruption—even something like a world-wide virus—can reveal an amazing truth about God. So far, we have discovered that God orchestrated all of the interruptions behind the scenes in Moses's life. Today in Exodus 3:1–22 we are going to see that God literally steps into the life of Moses in a miraculous way and shifts his course once again. This God, who Moses met at the burning bush, is our God today. When our world shifts, may we choose to look at God and discover the truth about who He is and what He wants for us.

If you grew up in church, you might be able to picture the artwork right now. Moses, sandal-less, bowing down to a shrubbery on fire. But the story is more marvelous than our Sunday school teachers could convey.

When God appeared to Moses, He wanted to move him to a new place. This was Moses's ultimate calling for his life. But God doesn't need to call us from a burning bush to reveal His plan to us. As we will see from Moses, our callings have little to do with us and more to do with God's promises and presence.

Before we get started, remember that the events in our lives are never wasted. God's sovereign plan for Moses's life included forty years of living as a shepherd. Those ordinary moments of growing a family and watching sheep were just as important as what God was going to call him to do next.

COVID might have picked you up and put you down in a new place. And if that is you today, I encourage you to read Moses's story in this chapter with a renewed hope. God has plans and a purpose. Because this event in Moses's life covers several verses, we are going to go through the biblical text and read it with eyes ready to answer this question:

Who is God?

Moses had spent time in Egypt learning and studying all of the Egyptian gods. He likely was taught by his Hebrew family of the God of Abraham, Isaac, and Jacob. Even with this, Moses had yet to come to a full knowledge of the one true God. There is a reason this event is significant in Moses's life. Not only was it a complete disruption, but God was going to finally keep His promise to redeem the Israelites.

As we study this meeting between Moses and God, may we look beyond the interruption to see the plans of God. In our most desperate disruptions, God does not leave us without the truth of His sovereign goodness. Come with me as we walk through Moses's conversation with the God of the universe and see how this God reaches into the heart of a man and shows him, and us, this amazing truth.

Holiness and Fire

> Now Moses was tending the flock of Jethro his
> father-in-law, the priest of Midian. And he led the
> flock to the back of the desert, and came to Horeb,
> the mountain of God. And the Angel of the LORD
> appeared to him in a flame of fire from the midst
> of a bush. So he looked, and behold, the bush was
> burning with fire, but the bush was not consumed.
> (Exod. 3:1–2)

The first thing we see in Exodus 3:1–2 is that God suddenly, abruptly, and without warning appears to Moses. A bush that didn't burn. A bush is a normal thing, but a fire that doesn't burn it up? This was not natural. This was a miracle.

Branches and wood catch on fire, then they turn into ash. The bush Moses saw was surviving the fire. The fire was not consuming the branches. The bush's fire could have signified God's purification of this particular place. Moses had probably passed by this area several times. The burning bush that was not consumed signified God's holy presence in our ordinary lives. Maybe God was telling Moses that this was going to be holy ground.

For centuries, and even today, fire is known to purify. God comes to Moses as a burning fire to possibly remind Moses of His holiness and the process of sanctification. The fire wasn't hurting or destroying, it was refining. Why? Because the first thing God tells Moses from the bush reveals what God values when someone approaches Him. God says:

"Do not draw near this place. Take your sandals
off your feet, for the place where you stand is holy
ground." (Exod. 3:5)

Before Moses had time to respond, God called Moses to recognize God's holiness. God is holy first and foremost. Just as the
angels in heaven declare, "Holy, Holy, Holy," we are reminded that
our God is first holy.

As a sign of respect, God asked Moses to remove his sandals.
God is a God of holiness. We as humans are tainted with sin, even
those of us who have accepted Christ as our Savior have sinful
natures we battle daily. A reminder of God's holiness is crucial as
we began to see Him more clearly in our disruptions.

Relationship and Identity

I am the God of your father—the God of Abraham,
the God of Isaac, and the God of Jacob. (Exod. 3:6)

Before God tells Moses anything more, He identifies Himself to
Moses. Moses doesn't know what or who this burning bush is, but
God doesn't leave him in the dark. Instead of telling Moses right
away who He is, God reveals His relationship with Moses. God uses
a phrase Moses would eventually write throughout the book of
Genesis: "I am the God of Abraham, Isaac, and Jacob."

Later in the conversation God will call Himself "I AM" which
means the self-sustaining one. God is surely self-sustaining and
transcendent, above all of us here on earth. God didn't relate to

Moses in that way yet; instead God reminded Moses of the personal relationship He has had with His people.

Although we serve a God who is all-consuming, holy, and separate from us, God also draws near to us and shows us that He desires a relationship with us. Don't miss this in your doubts, displacements, and disillusionment. God wants you to know Him. He is closer than you could imagine and cares for you in an individual way.

Sorrow and Silence

> And the LORD said: "I have surely seen the oppression of My people who are in Egypt, and have heard their cry because of their taskmasters, for I know their sorrows. . . . Now therefore, behold, the cry of the children of Israel has come to Me, and I have also seen the oppression with which the Egyptians oppress them." (Exod. 3:7, 9)

I love that the very first thing God tells Moses is, "I have seen the suffering." God sees your suffering too. I pray you will know this truth deep inside your bones. I remember when COVID first hit, and panic and suffering were everywhere. We would all wake up each day to hear of more cases, more deaths, nurses stretched thin, and loved ones dying alone. God sees the suffering.

The Israelites had been crying out to God for decades. Generations had lived, worked, suffered, and died without one new prophetic word from God. When our world spins upside down, I don't know about you, but I have the tendency to feel as if God has suddenly just gotten so quiet.

Can you imagine the plight of the Israelites during this time? The service, the hard work, zero rights, and disregarded as trash. They were treated horribly, and God was silent. When we don't hear God right away, it is easy to believe that God is actually silent or He doesn't hear.

One day when my youngest was only two years old, he was riding in the seat at the front of the grocery cart. The entire trip around the store was filled with his talking. If an onlooker had noticed, I didn't say anything to him the whole time. I was giving him sweet kisses and eye contact every now and then, but I didn't respond to him verbally. I wasn't ignoring him. My silence didn't mean I wasn't listening. I could hear him and I cared for him, but I only responded when it felt necessary. I did this because I am his mother. I know him. I love him. My silence was not a reflection of my love. So it is with God.

We can take comfort in knowing God is not only listening, but when the time is right, He will always answer. In the meantime, we know His silence is not a reflection of His love for us. In the middle of our seasons of silence, God is in the pages of Scripture ready to comfort us and remind us of truth. I guarantee, from someone who has sought Him time and time again, He is there. When sorrow and silence are a part of your life, open your heart to His Word.

It is not just a cop-out answer. I have felt the silence of God many times. In my deepest pain I couldn't hear His voice, but I wasn't listening and wasn't looking in the right place. As soon as I began reading His Word, there was His voice. It takes time and sometimes it doesn't happen right away. I don't stop reading though. I still bend my ear to hear God's voice from His Word. Why? Because when I cry to God, I don't have to doubt whether He hears. I know He does.

> I love the LORD, because He has heard my voice
> and my supplications. (Ps. 116:1)

God tells Moses, "I have seen, I have heard, and I know . . ." In our sorrow when we face those things we didn't sign up for, we can believe that God sees us, hears us, and knows our hearts. Keep crying out to Him, because He listens.

A New Plan

> "Come now, therefore, and I will send you to Pharaoh that you may bring My people, the children of Israel, out of Egypt." (Exod. 3:10)

God's next words reveal a new plan for Moses's life. Whenever I think about my story and how God has rearranged the pieces over and over again, I have to remember that God always has a plan. God's sovereign plan is never off track, even if mine seems to be.

The God of the Bible doesn't react to the circumstances of life. God orchestrates them. He has destined a plan—and although the plan might feel new to us, it was His plan all along. Even if the world is shifting, God's plans are good. Even when the Israelites spent years suffering, God was always planning a rescue. Both Jacob and Joseph spoke these prophetic words about God's future rescue:

Then Israel [Jacob] said to Joseph, "Behold, I am dying, but God will be with you and bring you back to the land of your fathers." (Gen. 48:21)

Then Joseph took an oath from the children of Israel, saying, "God will surely visit you, and you shall carry up my bones from here." (Gen. 50:25)

By faith Joseph, when he was dying, made mention of the departure of the children of Israel, and gave instructions concerning his bones. (Heb. 11:22)

These men believed that God would bring them back, and nothing could stand in God's way. We are going to see in the next few chapters how God plans to rescue His people. It is amazing and spectacular. I can't promise God will step in and part the waters for you, but I can tell you God is making a path even here.

Maybe you feel like your plans are ruined, but God's plan is never ruined. Our new path is actually the path God had planned all along. Right now do I wish I lived in Honduras? Yes. Do I know what God has planned for my family? Not really. We had plans to stay in Honduras indefinitely. What I've worked through, even in the past few months, is that often I don't know the plan. But just because I don't know the whole plan doesn't mean God doesn't have one. We cannot always know the specific plans God has for us, but we can know that God's plan always involves redemption. A renewing of your heart and mind is waiting. There will be seasons of redemption.

When we adopted our second child from China, we were told he might have a severe medical condition. After walking two years with our daughter's special needs, we prepared our hearts for the worst. When we returned home the doctors confirmed he was completely healthy.

Things I wish I could have done with our daughter, feelings and reactions I wish I could go back and change, I was able to do with our son. So much of his story felt like a redemption at the time. God took something really scary and traumatic—adopting from China—and turned it into something beautiful.

Today we have two children from China and our daughter is thriving. She walks, is learning to talk, takes care of herself, and is even learning to read. She is bright, and graduating from high school doesn't seem impossible at all. I look at the faces of both of my children and see God's redemption. I cling to it as we face the unknown. We don't know how we will serve God as missionaries in the future. But God will redeem even the hurt we've experienced from leaving Honduras.

The Israelites needed redemption too. Moses was not to be the hero—God would be doing the rescuing. Don't look at people or jobs or ambitions to rescue you from disrupted plans. People will fail us and circumstances can constantly shift. The only one we can rely on to direct our paths is God. The wise king Solomon tells us,

> Trust in the LORD with all your heart,
> And lean not on your own understanding;
> In all your ways acknowledge Him,
> And He shall direct your paths. (Prov. 3:5–6)

Does it say we won't have hardships on this path? No. It says we will see God directing it when our hearts are trusting Him. God's plan for Moses and the Hebrew people will not look like they imagined, but we know their story, don't we? God is going to reveal, in a great and mighty way, His plan for them and it is good. Can we believe the same thing about our lives? Our God has not changed His character. We might not have frogs descend or water turn to blood, but God will make a way because His path for us is good.

Time and Space

> And God said to Moses, "I AM WHO I AM." And He said, "Thus you shall say to the children of Israel, 'I AM has sent me to you.'" Moreover God said to Moses, "Thus you shall say to the children of Israel: 'The LORD God of your fathers, the God of Abraham, the God of Isaac, and the God of Jacob, has sent me to you. This is My name forever, and this is My memorial to all generations.'" (Exod. 3:14–15)

For the first time in Scripture God tells us what His name is. All throughout Genesis, people had names for God. Moses wrote God's name in Genesis 1 as *Eliom*, which means "Creator, Almighty God." That name fits with the account of creation. Surely our God is all-powerful, and when it comes to God's plans for Egypt, He will reveal Himself as all-powerful. God is also personal. He is named the God of Abraham, Isaac, and Jacob because God is not just a God over an entire nation, He is concerned even for the individual.

God tells Moses that he is a personal God and is very much present. God is a God of right now. He tells Moses, "I AM . . . I am the God of . . ." These are present-tense verbs. Abraham, Isaac, and Jacob lived in the past. Moses did not know these men. In fact, it had been generations since these men lived. But their God was a God of the present. Moses needed to know that this God would be present in time and space.

Times have changed, but God will never change. What a comfort to know that even in the midst of our world shifting, God will never change. He will always be "I AM." Psalm 46:1 says, "God is our refuge and strength, a very present help in trouble." This word *present* holds the connotation of "well-proved." God has been proven to be near to us both in time and space. We are reminded, with Moses, that God's very name means He is close.

Do you need to know God is present? Do you feel like your version of God is distant? Do you need to know that our all-powerful and personal God is both present physically, right here with you, but also present in this current time? We do not live in the times of Abraham, Isaac, and Jacob. Nor did Moses. But we also do not live in the time of Moses. We are thousands of years removed, but time is nothing to God.

Power and Promise

"So I will stretch out My hand and strike Egypt with all My wonders which I will do in its midst; and after that he will let you go." (Exod. 3:20)

God gives Moses an outline of the plan. He tells Moses that amazing things are about to happen, and after this the Pharaoh will let the people go. In the next chapter we are going to look at Moses's response to God's revelation and calling. God gives Moses more details as the two of them have a conversation, but here we see that God has given Moses two things to rest on. The first is God's power.

God would use plagues to reach in and show His power, but what if we marveled at the power of God evident in our lives today? Think of the way animals live and survive. God has intricately designed each one to live, take care of its young, and survive in their environment. My son was reading a book about beavers yesterday. We talked about how they build dams and know exactly how to do it! Who taught them? As we watched a beaver on a video carrying sticks and mud to build his home I marveled at the precious love and care God gave these creatures to allow them to know how to survive.

The vastness of space brings me to my knees before a wonderfully powerful God. Even with all the technology man has created, we have yet to come to the end of the universe. We can sing with the psalmist, "How great is our God!"

The second thing God gives Moses here is a promise. God says, "He [Pharaoh] will let you go . . ." It was a fact. Even man's hardness of heart could not foil God's promise to free His people. God has given us promises from Scripture. Things like He will never leave us, He will provide all we need, and He is going to be close to us. No amount of sin, darkness, or sorrow can foil these promises.

COVID changed a lot of things, but it did not change God. The things you are facing might have changed your life, but they did not change God. We can know God as a powerful and personal God because of His Son, Jesus.

Jesus and Moses

The life of Jesus reflects the idea of God's personal and powerful presence. Jesus not only brings this idea to light, He demonstrates to us how we can live our lives practically with this knowledge. First, we know Jesus was called Emmanuel, which means God with us. God would come down to live and breathe, 100 percent man in the Person of Jesus Christ.

> And the Word became flesh and dwelt among us,
> and we beheld His glory, the glory as of the only
> begotten of the Father, full of grace and truth.
> (John 1:14)

Jesus spent His life drawing near to those around Him. He touched them. He healed them. The miracles of Jesus demonstrate His ability to walk among us, understand our suffering, and speak into our lives.

> Then He [Jesus] came to Bethsaida; and they
> brought a blind man to Him, and begged Him
> to touch him. So He took the blind man by the
> hand . . . (Mark 8:22–23)

The message of Jesus is that God's presence is both powerful and personal. Jesus was powerful enough to dispel demons, heal the blind, the lame, and the sick. In all of this He drew near to us.

At the burning bush Moses encountered a God who sees, hears, and knows us. God has a plan for our lives. He is present right now with us and His power and promises will come to pass. We might not be able to see it, but we can look at the life of Moses as a whole to know God did have a plan for him. If God had a plan for Moses's life, He has a plan for mine. And for your life as well. It doesn't mean we will always understand, but we can bring our concerns to God. Even when God revealed Himself to Moses, as we will see, Moses still had questions. God sees and has a purpose for us, but He also invites us into a relationship with Him so we can ask questions.

Prayer

Dear God of the fathers who have come before me, all my life You have been faithful and good. Let me believe that You are holy, personal, and powerful because You deeply care about me. The life I'm living feels upside down and sometimes I just want to go back. Remind me that You were there in the past and You will not leave me now. You have a plan and Your plan is never ruined. It is always on time. Help me believe that today. Amen.

 Resting in God's Goodness

After looking at the characteristics of God in this chapter, circle which one means the most to you right now in your season:

Holy God

Personal God

God who sees

Powerful God

Read these verses about God being both personal and powerful. Write down what you notice.

Psalm 9:9–10

Psalm 34:17–18

Psalm 46:7

Psalm 70:4–5

Psalm 138:6

One of the most unique aspects about our God, compared to other gods, is that He is both personal and powerful. It doesn't make sense to have a God who is both beyond what we can imagine but chooses to be close enough to us to know our names. What about this aspect of God brings comfort to your heart? How is God's proactive nature a comfort to you?

_____

_____

6

God, What Are You Doing?

Moving to Honduras was not a choice my husband and I made lightly. Nor was our path a straight line to get there. God had to interrupt our life in a few ways in order to lead us. When we experienced a particular closed door, we questioned what God was doing. Even as my husband and I face another closed door now, we realize God's plan has not been interrupted.

As a young girl I believed God had called me to be a missionary. I didn't know what that would look like, but it was all I talked about as a child. Several times during my teenage and college years I surrendered my life to God and told Him I was willing to go and do anything He wanted me to do. When I met my husband, he had not been called or felt the pull toward missions personally, but God opened his heart, apart from me. While we were dating, Jason surrendered to God to serve wherever God would lead us.

After getting married we went to several mission's conferences and spent time talking to various mission boards. The answer was always, "Pay off your school loan debt and then we can talk." My husband was just finishing residency as a doctor, so there were quite a bit of loans to pay off. After residency, he accepted a job in a rural clinic. It was located forty minutes from our house. For a few years he drove to one of the poorest counties in our state and saw patients at a government subsidized clinic. In return the government helped pay off half of his school loans.

Some years later my husband was asked to join a private practice to work alongside another pediatrician. First he would work as an employee, but over time could possibly become a partner. My heart leaped with joy. This was my husband's dream job. It seemed as if God was leading us to this practice, but we were hesitant. If Jason signed on as a partner, there would be no full-time mission work. He might get to travel a few weeks out of the year, but we would not be moving overseas. Having a private practice takes a lot of work, and time off would be rare. We prayed and fasted for a whole month. We asked God, "Do you want us as full-time missionaries or just part-time?"

At the end of that month, God didn't speak from heaven or give us a sign. So Jason accepted the job. After a few months we suspected the business was not going well. Jason was not nearly as busy as they thought he would be. It turned out the practice didn't have enough patients to support two doctors. Because Jason was the employee, the owner decided to let Jason go. Unfortunately, it was really bad timing and he didn't give us much warning. It seemed like this job was hand-picked to fit both my husband's desires and abilities, but now God was closing the door.

We spent the first weekend after we found out mourning what we thought would be his last and perfect job. It was a process of sadness on many levels. Another job opened up, but in the medical field it takes a several weeks to be able to start, and I watched my husband stay home for two months. The position he accepted was at our local hospital. It wasn't the job he would have picked out, but God was still leading, even though we felt lost.

The closed door turned out to be the answer. During the two months between jobs, we prayed and asked God for direction. We were reminded of our prayers and fasting a few months prior. As we talked about the job transfer, we asked the question: Maybe full-time missionary work was one of God's purposes for our life? God moved in our hearts, and we began looking more seriously into moving overseas. Turns out this new job was perfect for this. His schedule allowed for travel as we raised support.

Five years later we sold our house, our belongings, and packed up our lives to move to Central America. It was January 2020. God had led us there. We were so excited to walk with God on this exciting new adventure.

You know what happened next. COVID shut down the world and shut down our plans. Every single plan we had for our mission work in Honduras was canceled. Instead, we found ourselves homesick, alone, not attending church in person, and navigating not only a third-world country, but a third-world country with intense COVID restrictions. Oh, and we didn't speak Spanish. Two and half years later, after getting settled and comfortable, God decided to move us again. Another closed door. I'll share more about this part of our story in a later chapter, but we suddenly found ourselves with more questions. This was not what we had signed up for.

Questions are a natural response to change. Moses responded to the burning bush and God's new plan for His life with questions. God knows we are just human, and I love that God does not shy away from our questions.

Maybe you've asked God questions when you looked at your life. It might have been the first thing you did when a hard thing happened. When life is uprooted and suddenly God has thrown in a plot twist, it is okay if we ask questions. He understands. We can have a conversation with Him, even after devastating loss and complete disruption. He is willing to listen to our questions. Sometimes the answers aren't what we expect, but we know He hears us.

Who Am I?

The conversation at the burning bush reveals so much about the God who is near to us. After God makes His announcement to deliver His people and use Moses in this mighty way, Moses speaks up. Instead of just walking away, Moses stays to ask four questions. The first question was about Moses's identity. Although forty years prior he had been ready to be the leader, not any more. Who was Moses, to lead God's people?

> But Moses said to God, "Who am I that I should go to Pharaoh, and that I should bring the children of Israel out of Egypt?" (Exod. 3:11)

Moses is basically saying, "Why me?" The world's answer would be something like, "You are more than enough! God is calling you. You must be special simply because you have been asked to do this great thing." Instead, we see God's answer to the question:

> So He [God] said, "I will certainly be with you." (3:12)

The answer isn't "you're enough," the answer is "God's presence is enough." Moses would not go into Egypt alone nor would he spend any time leading the people of Israel by himself. God would go with him. When God calls us out of something, we can remember God doesn't ever leave us.

What Do I Do?

The second question Moses asks is "What will I say?" It seems Moses has accepted God's call, but now it comes to the next step. What will Moses say to the people of Israel? What if they don't listen?

> Then Moses said to God, "Indeed, when I come to the children of Israel and say to them, 'The God of your fathers has sent me to you,' and they say to me, 'What is His name?' what shall I say to them?" (v. 13)

Moses wants to know exactly how the plan will work. What is he to say? How would he say it? Once again, we look at God's response: "And God said to Moses, "I AM WHO I AM" (v. 14).

In other words, God is all-sufficient, all-powerful, and in need of nothing. God is telling Moses that He will not only give Moses the words, but God will make the people listen. Self-sufficiency is not biblical. God requires us to work *with* Him, not necessarily *for* Him. Moses would see success this time because God would make them hear him: "Then they will heed your voice" (Exod. 3:18).

This is the first time the name Yahweh is mentioned in the Bible. This is God's covenant-keeping name associated with God's loving-kindness and goodness. When we ask what's next or what to do, we can remember who God is. "I am who I am" means I am all that you need me to be. God is everything we could ever want or need. It would be God's hand saving His people.

Do you find yourself saying, "God, I don't know how this is going to work out. I didn't prepare for this"? My husband's job transition and later our transition back to the States came at times when life seemed in transition already. How would we move forward? But it was God who was moving. God provided more than enough during that time to complete not one but two adoptions. When we moved back to the States, we didn't know how things would work out. But God showed us again and again He would provide.

> "So I [God] will stretch out My hand and strike Egypt with all My wonders which I will do in its midst; and after that he will let you go. And I will give this people favor in the sight of the Egyptians; and it shall be, when you go, that you shall not go empty-handed." (Exod. 3:20–21)

How will we face this new life, this new calling, or this new set of circumstances? How will we do it? We remind ourselves God is in need of nothing, and He is with us. If God's great sovereignty has brought us here, His great power will see us through it. God will do it. God's provision and power will accomplish His will.

What If?

After asking what he is to say, Moses asked God, "What if this happens?" I think Moses was still a little nervous about going up to the Israelites and telling them he was to lead them out of Egypt.

> Then Moses answered and said, "But suppose they will not believe me or listen to my voice; suppose they say, 'The LORD has not appeared to you.'" (Exod. 4:1)

God gives Moses a sign. First, God turns a broken branch into a snake. And remember, all this time the bush is still burning. Moses probably didn't take the stick from the fire, but a regular branch just lying around in the dust and dirt. What a symbol of Moses himself. God seems to say, "If I can do a wonderful miracle with an ordinary branch, I can use you, Moses, an ordinary man."

The next sign is turning Moses's hand leprous and then healing him in one swift movement. God shows Moses that the way this is going to work is it will be God's hand to strike Egypt—Moses need only be a servant willing to obey.

Questions and Doubt

We can have questions, but they must not lead us down the path of doubt. Doubt is never the way. When we returned home from Honduras, I doubted. I doubted God's plan, and even that He had one. It was very disorienting. Friend, we do not have to live in doubt. Yes, we are invited to question God, but lingering in doubts and fears will lead us nowhere. We can combat doubt with truth about God's character. Moses was afraid, worried, and doubted whether this was really what God wanted him to.

In the middle of Moses's questions, God responded with two miracles. He turned a branch into a snake. Then He caused Moses's hand to be covered in leprosy and cleansed it right away. What was the purpose of these signs? To show Moses that although God was going to use him, the power behind everything belonged to God.

God asked Moses to get a stick, a normal stick lying around. Those sticks probably littered the ground where Moses walked every day. God can use even the most ordinary thing to show His glory. When Moses's hand became leprous, this shows us that God is sovereign over our very bodies. God determines a man's worth and ability because God created that man.

When we start to question God, may we look to Him for answers—not in doubt, but in faith. There is a difference between my children asking in doubt and asking in faith. For example, as we drive in the car to the beach they might ask, "When will we get there?" or "Will I get to swim in the ocean today?" Those are questions that believe we will arrive at the beach sometime and eventually they will get to swim in the water. If they asked, "Are we even going?" or "What if we don't get to swim at all?" it would reflect their distrust in my promise to them.

Today we may not have God performing miracles for us to see with our eyes, but we do have the Word of God in our hands. In this chapter and especially in the next chapter, we will see how our God is so powerful that the mighty nation of Egypt would be brought low. We can be confident to trust this same God.

Can I Really Do This?

The final question Moses asked was rooted in fear. Moses says, "O my Lord, I am not eloquent, neither before nor since You have spoken to Your servant; but I am slow of speech and slow of tongue" (Exod. 4:10). Essentially Moses said to God, "I am not good enough. Can I really do this?"

Moses went back to his first question, "Who am I?" (Exod. 3:11). Moses really didn't feel qualified and God's answer turned the focus off of Moses and onto God. "You don't have to be qualified; I'm the one who will do it and I have created, called, and equipped you."

I love God's response to Moses:

> "Who has made man's mouth? Or who makes the mute, the deaf, the seeing, or the blind? Have not I, the LORD? Now therefore, go, and I will be with your mouth and teach you what you shall say." (Exod. 4:11–12)

When God called my husband and I out of our comfort zones to this new country and to these new people, we had many questions. But one that kept coming to our minds was this: "Who are *we*?" We are nothing special. Moses felt that way, and sometimes I think we all do. How can we move forward when life shifts?

God's response to our questions will often be, "This is who I am . . ." We want an answer to why, what, and how, but God says: "This is who I am and this is what I am going to do." God did not tell Moses every single plague or that the people would struggle to understand. God did not reveal details to Moses—and friends, often He does not show us the details either.

Even today I struggle with the mystery that is God's way. I don't always know the purpose in the pain or even the details of His plan, but I have come to see God in the middle of everything. We might not have the answers we want, but we can know God. He has made Himself known and we can learn to lean into our shifting stories because God is going to be mighty and faithful.

When you have questions for God because life isn't going how you planned, I hope you can see these truths: God's presence and plan are rooted in His love and power.

Who God Is

> And God said to Moses, "I AM WHO I AM." And He said, "Thus you shall say to the children of Israel, 'I AM has sent me to you.'" (Exod. 3:14)

Can you say that knowing God is enough? Who is this God of the Bible? As we move forward after a sudden plot twist and canceled plans, let's remind ourselves about God. Here in Exodus we see three things God is to us, especially when life is turned upside down.

God is sovereign. God is in control. Even when circumstances are not going "as planned," we can trust and hope in Him. We make conscious efforts to praise God. We choose to not let despair or fear take control of our minds. When our minds are focused on

God's sovereignty, our hearts will trust. *God is self-sufficient and transcendent.*

> For by Him all things were created that are in heaven and that are on earth, visible and invisible, whether thrones or dominions or principalities or powers. All things were created through Him and for Him. And He is before all things, and in Him all things consist. (Col. 1:16–17)

> But who is able to build Him a temple, since heaven and the heaven of heavens cannot contain Him? Who am I then, that I should build Him a temple, except to burn sacrifice before Him? (2 Chron. 2:6)

> "Can anyone hide himself in secret places,
> So I shall not see him?" says the LORD.
> "Do I not fill heaven and earth?" says the LORD.
> (Jer. 23:24)

Even though God is both completely sovereign and superior, God is also specific. God is not an abstract idea or concept. God is a Person. The words *I AM* are the Hebrew verb "to be." God is a Being, not a thought or theory or abstraction. Our God exists in a Person form. Because of this, He is able to be known. Our God—the transcendent and all-powerful, in-need-of-nothing God—stoops down to our level and speaks to us. God tells Moses that He is the God of a specific people. We have a God who is both powerful and personal.

What God Is Doing

"So I will stretch out My hand and strike Egypt with
all My wonders which I will do in its midst; and after
that he will let you go." (Exod. 3:20)

One of the things I love about God is that He has given us all
the information we need to trust Him. He does this with Moses as
He outlines a basic plan for how He will rescue His people. He tells
Moses He will be the one to do the work.

Although God does not speak to us as He did to Moses, and
gives few details, we can look at Scripture and see God at work in
our lives even today. I'm not saying God will come to you through
burning bushes, withered hands, snakes, or branches. I'm saying
God has given us His Word and even with a quick look we can see
how God is already working in our lives.

During our times of uncertainty, we can remember our sovereign and supreme God is intimately aware of us. When we find
ourselves asking God questions, let's respond to our hearts like
the psalmist in Psalm 77. In this psalm of lament, the author is crying out to God. He questions and mourns the path God has put
him on:

> I cried out to God with my voice—
> To God with my voice;
> And He gave ear to me. (Ps. 77:1)
>
> I will remember the works of the LORD;
> Surely I will remember Your wonders of old. . . .

You are the God who does wonders;
You have declared Your strength among the
peoples. (Ps. 77:11, 14)

God's work here in Exodus with Moses and the people of Israel are a reminder for us of God's great strength and love.

The God of Moses is our God today. How do we know this? Because Someone came hundreds of years after Moses who was the very presence of God with us. Jesus is the reason we can trust the God of Moses. The same God who spoke from the burning bush speaks through Jesus today.

Jesus and Moses

The Bible says in Matthew 1:18–24 that a man named Joseph from Nazareth was visited by an angel. The woman he was going to marry was pregnant. Because he was a good man, he was going to settle the issue quietly, without a public display. An angel told him in a dream to keep Mary as his wife because the Child she was carrying was from God.

In this dream Joseph was told the Child's name: Emmanuel. This name for Jesus means "God with us" (Matt. 1:23). As we saw in the previous chapter, our God came to us. Jesus entered this world as a baby. Jesus wrapped Himself in our human flesh, choosing to live a quiet and unassuming life. Our Savior came to earth to do more than just die for our sins. He came so we could know the very presence of God.

> God's delays aren't evidence of unconcern, for He
> hears our groans, sees our plight, feels our sorrows,
> and remembers His covenant.[5]—Warren Wiersbe

Moses saw the glory of God's presence burning bright in the fiery bush and believed God—even in the middle of questions—because God was going to be the Rescuer.

God's presence would be the key to the people's exodus from Egypt. When we face the unexpected, God's presence is what we need the most. Yes, we might have to walk wilderness seasons or feel the burning heat of unanswered questions. But even in this we can experience God's presence.

How is God in the middle of my day? I'm reheating coffee in the microwave. In the kitchen I hear the voices of my children talking softly. Is this God with me?

In the middle of the night as I rocked my child back to sleep, I didn't know if there would be a night I would sleep through without hearing a peep. Still, He was with me in this season. The children sleep through the night now, but I am awake filled with thoughts of heartache. Every season God has been present. It means He will be present today.

As the toaster pops up the frozen waffles and I fill their plates with breakfast, I pour syrup slowly—*Is God with me?* I wonder through a list of to-dos in my mind for this day. Still clouded with sleep, I wonder, *What does it mean? Emmanuel.*

Joseph and Mary knew the baby, the boy, the teenager, and then the man who would be their Savior. The Word of God made flesh, lived in their house, washed dishes, built tables, and cleaned up sawdust. The love of God in flesh and blood breathed the air I breathe and did the ordinary things I do every day.

The One who hung the stars and took the journey from heaven to earth is with me now. Some days I can feel His presence and some days I can't. But I hold onto truth with clenched fists. I welcome it like drinking from a cold water fountain, letting truth quench the thirst parching my soul.

God is faithful to meet me in the pages of His Word. My Savior knows my hurts. Grace and mercy are a part of my day. Jesus was touched with my pain and today He holds me up. God's answer is: I am with you.

And not only is God with us, He is going to work in our lives.

Moses gets a front row seat to God's amazing power when he returns to Egypt. Although we would love for God to step in and reveal His power like this, the events that happened thousands of years ago remind us that our God, sovereign and near to us, is still all-powerful. Remember, you don't need a God who is just sovereign. Nor do you need a God who is just good. You need a God who is both powerfully sovereign and powerfully good.

Prayer

Dear heavenly Father, there are times I feel like all I do is ask You questions. I know that You welcome me to speak to You, but during these difficult transitions and disrupted times, I confess I often feel like I'm wasting Your time with my questions. Remind me that You care for each of my doubts and You will speak truth to my heart.

Teach my heart the truth. Help me remember that You welcome my questions, but You also have answers for me in the pages of the Bible. Help me know Your wisdom, feel Your comfort, and see Your goodness today. Amen.

 Resting in God's Goodness

The presence of God isn't something we often think about, but He is ever with us. Describe what you believe the "presence of God" means in your own words.

_____

_____

_____

What do these passages tell us about God's presence?

Isaiah 57:15

Psalm 139:7

Psalm 16:11

Why do you think God didn't just tell Moses, "You can do this!"? Why is "I'll go with you . . ." a better answer to this statement: "I can't do this!"

God, why have You allowed _____ to happen in my life?

Instead of searching for an answer to that question, circle the answer that best fits this blank for you:

God, I want to learn more about Your _____ (faithfulness, mercy, love, compassion, sovereignty, goodness, forgiveness, comfort, and wisdom).

7

God's Power Revealed

While we were adopting our daughter, we had several specific answers to prayers. On one occasion God revealed His ability to work in the unseen. Once all of our paperwork was turned in, we had a period of waiting for a match. This meant that as files of children from China would enter our agency's email inbox, they would search the children's age, gender, and medical conditions to see if any of the waiting adoptive families would be a good fit for the child. My heart was anxious to be matched right away. But they told us to expect to wait three to nine months.

Every day I prayed that God would do it in two months. It felt impossible, but I believed God could do it. In His loving-kindness and amazing power, we were matched with our daughter in six weeks! I could list a hundred similar prayers and answers. Things I prayed happened much sooner than expected. As we walk with Moses out of Egypt, God is going to provide for His people, but first they needed to see His power. Before we take a step forward, sometimes we need to be reminded of God's amazing power that goes before us.

Through the series of the first nine plagues, we are going to see what Moses and the Hebrews needed to see: God's amazing power to orchestrate every aspect of their lives.

The Israelites were in a big mess, and redemption and deliverance were finally on the horizon. When Moses returned with Aaron to Egypt, he first met with the Israelite leaders. The two brothers performed miracles and the response was worship (Exod. 4:31). Next Moses and Aaron went in and told Pharaoh, "Thus says the LORD God of Israel, 'Let My people go, that they may hold a feast to Me in the wilderness'" (Exod. 5:1).

Notice each time Moses asked the Pharoah to let the people go, he said, "Let them go, so that they may serve." In other words, God didn't just want to free His people from slavery, but free them to worship and serve Him. God delivers us, not so we can be free to do whatever we want, but so we can be free to love and serve Him in the way we were created to do so.

In Exodus 5:2, Pharoah responded with, "Who is the LORD?" In other words, Pharaoh worshipped dozens of gods, but he had never heard of this Lord, Yahweh. This was a new God, and Pharaoh wasn't going to bow down to this God's wishes. Pharaoh's question was not one of curiosity. The question came from a heart that was arrogant. In other words, "Who does this God of Israel think He is?"

God answered Pharaoh in the next several chapters with the ten plagues. Concerning the first few plagues, the Bible says Pharaoh hardened his own heart (Exod. 7:13, 22; 8:15, 19, 32; 9:7), but then it says that God hardened Pharaoh's heart (Exod. 10:16–17). God used the first nine plagues, or signs, to answer the question, "Who is the LORD?" But God also did a work in Pharaoh's heart. God's desire is for all to come to repentance (2 Pet. 3:8–10), even Pharaoh. But Pharaoh would not bend.

F. B. Meyer says this:

> Let it never be forgotten that if we are told God hardened Pharaoh's heart and the heart of his servants, we are also told again and again that he hardened his own heart; and it is not difficult to understand how God may be described as doing what really was due to Pharaoh's resistance to the chain of providential dealings that were intended to enlighten and convert him.[6]

Instead of bending in humility, Pharaoh responded in pride. God had a purpose and plan for each of the plagues, but the overall point was to show Himself as the all-powerful one and only God. When our stories shift, we don't need to see the plan, we need to see God. At the burning bush God showed Moses that He was a God of a personal nature. He was a God with a name, who would be near to Moses.

As our paths twist and turn we might be able to accept that God is loving and good, but we doubt He is all-powerful. When we find ourselves in circumstances of pain and suffering, we need a God who is both good and sovereign. God reveals His ultimate sovereignty here in these verses.

After Moses and Aaron met with the Pharaoh, the people were punished with harder work. When this happened, they complained to Moses. They told him, "Let the LORD look on you [Moses] and judge, because you have made us [the Israelites] abhorrent in the sight of Pharaoh and in the sight of his servants, to put a sword in their hand to kill us" (Exod. 5:21). Moses didn't respond to the people but turned to God in his rejection. It seems Moses had learned how to run to God with his heartaches.

Moses seemed to ask, "God, why have you brought me here if this isn't even going to work?" In Exodus 6:1, the Lord said to Moses, "Now you shall see what I will do to Pharaoh." God went on to reveal part of His plan for Moses. Notice that God doesn't number the plagues nor does God outline exactly how He will deliver His people. God begins to list all of the things Moses needs to remember and know.

Moses repeats these promises to the people, but it says in Exodus 6:9 that because of their bondage and anguish they did not believe God. How often do we get so consumed with our circumstances that we fail to believe God will truly rescue us? God was not only going to judge the cruelty of the Egyptians, God was going to reveal His awesome power to His people who were so oppressed they failed to believe His promises.

The word for *plague* is actually the Hebrew word for *sign*. Although they were a form of judgment, these signs were also pictures. Remember, Pharaoh asked, "Who is Yahweh?" Moses also asked at the bush, "When the people ask who you are, what should I say?"

The signs or plagues were not random. God orchestrated them to condemn the gods of Egypt, reveal His power, and show Himself to the people. Some scholars believe each of the plagues correlated with a false god. For the first plague God turned the Nile River to blood. The lifeblood of Egypt was the Nile River, which flowed through the fertile fields of Egypt providing fish, water, and crops. God smote this first. The second plague was frogs. Today, archeologists have discovered many deity statues with frog-heads. More than anything, these animals brought a mess. The entire land stunk of frogs. Even in this, Pharaoh refused to budge. So, God inflicted the third plague, which was gnats or lice to demonstrate God's anger at the pride and stubbornness of Pharaoh. After this, God sent flies to ruin the land.

At this point Pharaoh offered a compromise. He said, "Go and serve God here in Egypt." But compromise is not obedience. So, God sent disease to beasts in the fifth plague and to mankind in the form of boils in the sixth plague. The hardness of not only Pharaoh's heart, but even the hearts of those around him is evident as God sends a powerful thunderstorm. Surely Egypt had seen spring storms, but this one was beyond what would have ever been there before. Scholars agree that the weather near Egypt would have never naturally had hail, thunder, or fire in such a magnitude. The remaining crops and livestock died. Economically, Egypt was brought to its knees.

The next two plagues, eight and nine, were locusts and darkness. The locusts devastated all of the green things. Nothing was left to eat. A famine was looming and then darkness. The very sun which they worshipped was darkened. Day became night. Pharaoh professed to repent, but then only offered another compromise.

After nine plagues the great Pharaoh of Egypt, who was thought to be like a god, was brought low by the power of Yahweh. Even in all of his pride, prestige, and position, God was able to humble the Pharaoh of Egypt. It was not Moses who brought about the plagues, but God. Moses was simply a servant of God, used to reveal God's power. Moses and Aaron spoke the name of Yahweh to Pharaoh, but he would not listen. His pride would be his destruction.

On that final night in Egypt, God was going to step in and perform a terrible miracle. We often think of God's miracles as positive things, but this would be devastating to the Egyptians. God foretold what would happen, "Then there shall be a great cry throughout all the land of Egypt, such as was not like it before, nor shall be like it again" (Exod. 11:6).

This would not be a cry of victory, but of defeat. This would not be a cry from the children of God, but from the enemies of God. For those who would not repent and bow their hearts in humility, God would bow them in anguish.

All nations, no matter the generation, are accountable to God. Everyone must offer to God something in exchange for their sins. God has prescribed what is necessary and that is blood. It is time for God to give a picture that would be used for the rest of history.

As our family faced the unknown of adoption, one of the most awesome ways God revealed His power was through financially providing for us. Each time we had an adoption fee due, God somehow provided the money. My husband would get an unexpected bonus at work. Some friends (or even strangers) would send checks to us. One time the exact amount we needed showed up in our bank account the same week we needed it. The power, patience, and protection of God anchored us as we walked through life's twists and turns.

The Power of God

"It shall be as a sign to you on your hand and as a memorial between your eyes, that the LORD's law may be in your mouth; for with a strong hand the Lord has brought you out of Egypt." (Exod. 13:9)

Living in the time of Moses during those months would have been very disorienting. Strange occurrences happened randomly for both the Israelites and the Egyptians. Frogs, bugs, and darkness covered the land. They never knew what was going to happen next! Even Moses didn't know from one plague to another what God was going to do. God didn't reveal His entire plan to Moses.

Other than the burning bush, Moses had yet to see the breadth and depth of God's amazing power. Not only did God reveal His power, He did so in miraculous ways. Each plague revealed that God was King over all creation. The God who created the rules of nature and animals can bend and manipulate those very rules to accomplish His will.

The God who separated the waters on the first day of creation turned the Nile River into a river of blood. Creatures, created by God, obeyed His commands. On the second day of creation God created the sky and He used His power to rain down hail, fire, and thunder in the land. The green grass and trees which God had brought forth on the third day were destroyed by locusts. The Bible says there was no green thing left in the land. On the fourth day of creation God said let the sun, moon, and stars shine in the sky. The ninth plague brought darkness to the land.

All living creatures were formed on the sixth day. Even they can be controlled by our God. Frogs, gnats, and flies ruined and made a mess of the lives of the Egyptians. The livestock died from disease during the fifth plague. Even our very bodies do not belong to us. The God who created man can inflict any kind of disease on us as He wishes. For the sixth plague, boils covered the bodies of all who lived in Egypt. In a culture obsessed with cleanliness, this plague was especially devastating.

God's power was the point. The psalmists agree:

> For I know that the LORD is great,
> And our Lord is above all gods. . . .
> He destroyed the firstborn of Egypt, both of man
>   and beast.
> He sent signs and wonders into the midst of you,
>   O Egypt,
> Upon Pharaoh and all his servants. (Ps. 135:5, 8–9)

> They did not remember His power:
> The day when He redeemed them from the
>   enemy,
> When He worked His signs in Egypt,
> And His wonders in the field of Zoan;
> Turned their rivers into blood,
> And their streams, that they could not drink.
> (Ps. 78:42–44)

Instead of waiting for God to remove us from our situations, we can take a step back and marvel at the power of God. God might not use His power to do what we want Him to do to fix our lives, but God's power is moving in ways we have no way of knowing. The psalmist reminds us to sing of these wonderful works so we can remember all that God has done. Our God is still just as powerful today as He was in the time of Moses. Let's rest in this truth. We can trust our all-powerful God to step in when and how He wills.

The Patience of God

The LORD is slow to anger and great in power,
And will not at all acquit the wicked. (Nah. 1:3)

Through all of the signs and plagues of Egypt, it is the patience of God that strikes me as so compassionate. Yes, there were judgments. God's goal was to deliver His people, but in every single hardship both for the Egyptians and the Israelites, God revealed patience.

God sent signs and plagues and it took months and months. Not for His sake, and not just to demonstrate His power, but to demonstrate His patience with sinners. Many people have this idea that the God of the Old Testament was a revengeful, wrathful God. The ten plagues are used to prove their point. But the Bible does not give us this picture. Instead, God's patience shines through. It is said several times in the Bible, when describing God, that He is, "slow to anger."

But You, O LORD, are a God merciful and gracious,
Slow to anger and abounding in steadfast love
and faithfulness. (Ps. 86:15 ESV)

Just because God is slow to anger, doesn't mean He doesn't execute judgment as well. We see both His mercy and justice here in Exodus and the life of Moses. God was teaching Moses that even though sinners deserved punishment, God is willing to wait and give them an opportunity to repent.

> The Lord is not slack concerning His promise, as some count slackness, but is longsuffering toward us, not willing that any should perish but that all should come to repentance. (2 Pet. 3:9)

God is not willing that any—even the very enemies of His people, the Egyptians and Pharaoh—would perish. What we see as God's punishment is actually God's grace, giving us time to repent, to get to know Him, and seek Him. The circumstances you find yourself in today might feel like God is punishing you. What if instead you saw them as opportunities to run to Him and rest?

As we walk this path, littered with unexpected detours, it is tempting to say, "God is not delivering me from this!" Instead, we can rejoice that our God gives us enough grace, enough strength, and enough joy to find Him even in this season. It starts with believing that our God is a God of patience.

The Protection of God

> As for God, His way is perfect;
> The word of the LORD is proven;
> He is a shield to all who trust in Him. (Ps. 18:30)

The ultimate punishment and judgment that would come on Egypt was the tenth and final plague. Plagues four through nine were not executed in the land where the Israelites lived, but this final plague would pass through their land as well as Egypt. God said there would be a "great cry" of anguish and sorrow. The result of sin and the punishment for rebellion is death, even for God's people.

God was going to execute judgment on the people of the land because they were guilty. Both Israelite and Egyptian were guilty before a holy God. The word *execute* means to do work or prepare. God requires a payment for sin, but He also provides the payment. God's wrath on the land was going to be severe, but God did not leave the people without a way to be protected.

If the lamb's blood covered the doorpost, God would pass over because of the blood. The blood of the lamb stood as a sentry, a guard, and a protection. All of the people in that house deserved death. God's judgment was death. But God's protection was also there. Even though it was available for all, not all would choose to accept it. When we face plot twists, we have protection. God secures and is a shield to all who trust Him. Will we see God's protection in our lives?

Protection doesn't always promise us safety. God doesn't promise safety, but that we will be protected in the end and our souls will not be lost in death. If something painful has entered your life, it is only because He permits it. Because we believe in the goodness of God, we can trust His sovereignty when life doesn't feel good. Did Moses know how God was going to work redemption? No, and neither do we. We might not know how, but God always provides a way.

Faith and Redemption

> By faith he [Moses] kept the Passover and the sprinkling of blood, lest he who destroyed the firstborn should touch them. (Heb. 11:28)

In all of our circumstances, good and bad, God requires of us this one thing: faith. Why does the author of the book of Hebrews tell us that Moses demonstrated faith when he kept the Passover? Why was Moses mentioned and not the entire congregation of Israel? Many would argue that Moses had faith in the coming Christ. He foresaw Jesus in this act of the Passover. The author of Hebrews doesn't say Moses had faith in Jesus, but says Moses had faith in God.

When they sprinkled the blood on the doorposts, the effects of it didn't take place right away. They sprinkled them at twilight. God's angel would not come until midnight. The act of faith was doing something and believing something before the end result.

Moses told the people to do this sprinkling of the blood with authority because Moses believed God's word. Moses did not hesitate to believe God. And so it must be with us today. Do we believe God's words, spoken to us through the Bible, that He will redeem and restore and deliver us? If we believe, we have faith. Faith was Moses's foundation and it can be ours as well.

This long, waiting season where you don't see the end is where faith is grown. This hard season when life feels like a series of deaths, it requires faith. Faith often grows best this way. Because our faith is not rooted in the end result, our faith is rooted in the One who speaks the Word. Redemption is about God. What we can learn about God during our time of suffering is key. God is all-powerful, so very patient, and our protector. God uses these times, however long they might last, to grow our faith.

Jesus and Moses

"Behold! The Lamb of God who takes away the sin of the world!" (John 1:29)

The Passover found in Exodus 12 was a picture of Jesus Christ. He was called by John the Baptist as the "Lamb of God" in John 1:29. This was a reference to the Passover lamb here in Exodus. Jesus would be the perfect lamb, spotless and sin-free. He would then be killed on a cross at the age of thirty-three. His blood would be spilled on the hill above the city of Jerusalem.

The lambs in the Old Testament would only cover and not cleanse all of the sins. We needed a more perfect sacrifice. That is why God instituted the Passover ritual for the people of Israel. It had to be repeated year after year. For hundreds of years animals' blood would be used to cover over sin. It was not enough.

But as we see in the passage below, Christ provides eternal redemption.

Not with the blood of goats and calves, but with His own blood He entered the Most Holy Place once for all, having obtained eternal redemption. For if the blood of bulls and goats and the ashes of a heifer, sprinkling the unclean, sanctifies for the purifying of the flesh, how much more shall the blood of Christ, who through the eternal Spirit offered Himself without spot to God, cleanse your conscience from dead works to serve the living God? (Heb. 9:12–14)

Jesus was born to a woman, lived a perfect life, was tempted to sin, but without sin. And then came the Passover. Jesus spent His last Passover celebration in an upper room shining a light on what would come. The darkness of our sin cannot outshine the Resurrection and the Life who is Jesus Christ.

As we look at our lives and whisper to ourselves, "I didn't sign up for this," we can trust that Jesus has walked the road of redemption for us. Providing the way, paving the way, and walking in the way we should walk. Jesus's life on the surface was filled with twists and turns, but the path led to our redemption. Jesus is the way of redemption, the foundation for our redemption, and the example of our redemption. Let us rest and trust Christ today. Even with our detours, God is leading us toward redemption.

One morning, I was up before the children, drinking my coffee in our house in West Virginia. I asked God, "What do You want me to see right now?" My heart still ached with the pain of leaving Honduras. My tears were still fresh from crying last night because I missed my friends. As I sat there, pondering, I realized a truth I tell people all the time. God redeems. He provided a home, a job for my husband, and a place to serve for our family. God was redeeming all the previous hurt we experienced from having to leave the mission field in such a harsh way.

This doesn't mean God will give us back everything we think we have lost, but He will use those broken pieces of our interrupted and devastated lives to build something new. God will restore. As we move with Moses away from Egypt, we are going to see God doesn't ask us to walk alone. No longer do we need to fear the future. We can cultivate peace in our hearts.

God is powerful enough to make a way, even if there seems to be no way. If you still doubt God is leading you, walk with Moses right up to the Red Sea and watch God deliver His people. Walking into the unknown allows you to deepen your faith in a God who is more powerful than you could ever imagine.

Prayer

O Jesus, be with me today as I remember that You have paid the price for my sin. With You I have peace with God and eternal life. Not only that, You are still working in my life. If there is breath in my lungs You are still working. You have not forgotten me and You have a plan. Even though the way seems daunting, and I don't know where You are leading, let me trust that You have provided redemption and You will not leave me now. Amen.

Resting in God's Goodness

Take a moment to read Exodus 12:1–28. The Passover was a unique time in the history of Israel, but even thousands of years later reading about this event is so amazing. Think about what the Israelites had to do. What was required of them?

_____

_____

_____

One important thing was faith. When we face the unknown, faith must be the foundation. It keeps us steady because it helps us focus on God, not our circumstances.

As we think about our lives, we can respond to suffering with discouragement if we forget God's power. What do these verses tell us about God's power and goodness?

1 Peter 1:3

Psalm 62:11–12

Isaiah 40:28–31

Walking the Invisible Road

My inner dialogue for 2015 was, *I didn't sign up for this.* After bringing home our daughter from China, the impossible task of moving into a new routine felt overwhelming. How would I juggle everything our daughter needed, plus meet the needs of our other three children? As the days inched by, I felt the weight of the hopeless task of living one more day. My husband and I seemed to fight about everything that year. I had signed up for adoption, but I didn't think or even imagine it would have such a lasting impact on every aspect of my life. I didn't sign up for *that.* Before I knew it, I had fallen headlong into depression.

Wearily, I confronted each day. Life wore me down until I felt like I was sinking. I was tired and angry. In particular, I found myself angry about drool. Never in my life would I have thought I would be mad about drool. All babies do it. But this was different. Drool suddenly became my #1 enemy. My daughter drooled much more than the average child, and I was powerless to stop it. I hated it when she would drool through the cutest outfits. Her bibs were always wet and cold around her neck, which caused a permanent red rash. No amount of wiping would keep her neck dry. She couldn't help it, but that didn't keep it from irritating me.

Eventually, I realized the drool represented all I had lost. I had pictured a little girl with lots of smiles and adorable long black hair who just needed a little love. I expected her to be like a newborn baby, who instantly loves and soothes. Instead, she would cry for hours, rejecting any of my comfort. She struggled to sit up, play, or even engage with any of us.

Have you ever looked at something in your life and said, "How could this be good? Where is God leading?" What is in your life today that makes you say, "I didn't sign up for *this*?" Is it a sudden job loss, a divorce, a death, or an illness? You had dreams and now they are broken. You thought God would rescue you, but now you find yourself saying, "This isn't how life is supposed to be."

The path of life isn't always clear and this is when God asks us to walk by faith. To walk with faith means we don't always see the way ahead, but we keep moving forward anyways. We have faith in our good and loving God. We choose to believe God is still in control. God is leading, and we can trust God to be working. Even though we would like to know where this road will lead, God says, "Trust Me and take the next step."

The children of Israel found themselves in the same situation, and surely Moses felt a little lost as well. As we saw in the previous chapter, God had done ten amazing miracles, but suddenly freedom looked out of reach for the former slaves. Right as the Israelites reached the Red Sea, Pharaoh changed his mind and gathered his army. The Israelites hadn't even gotten to the place where they were going to worship God when an impossible situation arrived. They'd left Egypt, but now Egypt was coming to kill them. They'd gotten themselves trapped between the sea and a huge army—and God had led them there. I'm sure many of them whispered (or cried out), *"I didn't sign up for this!"*

They saw the deep waters of the sea and the fierce army coming after them and they cried out to Moses. But what could he do? He was just a man. Maybe Moses was as upset as they were. What was God thinking leading them there? If we didn't know the rest of the story (and Moses didn't at the time), we would surely be questioning God. Hopelessness will do that to you.

When our story shifts unexpectedly, we usually begin to question two things: God's plan and God's power. Sometimes the hardest part about facing an impossible situation is knowing God was the one who allowed it. Just as God led the Israelites to this impossible place, God will sometimes allow us to fall into a situation that seems impossible to escape. That first year home with our daughter, this question plagued me: Why had He clearly led our family to adopt, only to lead us on this really hard, seemingly impossible path afterward?

If we are honest with each other, we can admit we've all asked God, "why" at some point in our lives. Men and women in the Bible were no exception. They asked why. Even today I still struggle when God's plan doesn't align with what I think is "good."

As we read through the Red Sea story in Exodus 14, it is easy for us to skip down to when God parts the water. But let's sit on the other side of the beach with Moses and the Israelites. Let's unpack a few things before the sea opens up with salvation.

After leaving Egypt, the newly freed people marched in the direction of the Red Sea. Although Exodus 13:18 says they were equipped for battle, they had never fought a war before. They encamped at the edge of the wilderness (Exod. 13:20) while God led them with a pillar of fire at night and a pillar of cloud during the day (Exod. 13:21–22). During this time, Moses surely didn't know God's plan, nor did the people. Instead of seeing the Red Sea as a place of rest, they looked back to see an army coming after them!

This impossible situation was a wall of water on one side and an army on the other. What is their first response? They said to Moses, "Didn't we tell you! We told you this would be impossible and you didn't listen to us. Now we are going to die!" (Exod. 14:12).

The blame game had started. I'm familiar with this game, which showed up pretty quickly in my own struggle as well. At first I blamed the orphanage, then I blamed our adoption agency, then I blamed my husband because he was calm through it all. Finally, I blamed God. I knew He was sovereign, but this didn't feel good. I had thought God was fair, but this didn't seem fair.

Blame feels good in the moment, because it allows us to project our anger and fear onto someone else. But blame leads pretty quickly to other emotions: doubt and worry. Those two little words can cause such panic and hopelessness if we let them dwell in our hearts. Once I was done blaming, I worried God's plan would be too hard for me. I doubted God's power to make things better. Did the Israelites as well? In Exodus 14:10 (ESV), it says, "they feared greatly." They doubted Moses as a leader and God as their Savior, which led to panic. One thought or a moment of doubt or worry isn't the problem; we all have doubts and worry about things on occasion. But when those things consume our minds, it leads us down a path of despair.

How can we avoid falling into despair? As we continue to unpack the Israelites' story here at the Red Sea, we are going to see how God demonstrates His power in a variety of ways—suggesting that disrupted plans are never the end of the story. We can trust God to lead us through the impossible situation—by allowing Him to change us. As we view this story through the eyes of Moses, we will see how he and the people of Israel were changed after this event. Yes, they still struggled and would sin again, but this event marked the pinnacle of their redemption and the beginning of their faith in God.

When suddenly we face the impossible, it is time for us to realize God might be bringing us to this situation to teach us that what seems impossible actually solidifies our belief in God and His goodness.

What the enemy might have meant for evil, would actually grow my faith in ways it never would have otherwise. The impossible shift in our story can reveal that God's power fights for us, His presence protects us, and a deeper faith can change us.

The Path of Nonaction

And Moses said to the people, "Do not be afraid. Stand still, and see the salvation of the LORD, which He will accomplish for you today. For the Egyptians whom you see today, you shall see again no more forever. The LORD will fight for you, and you shall hold your peace." (Exod. 14:13–14)

The Israelites had cried out to God, and as Pharaoh "drew near," they realized death was coming. There would be no escape. They would not return to slavery; they would simply be slaughtered there by the sea. In moments of panic, it is good to cry out to God, but when we do, we sometimes miss His response. We cry out and ask God to help us, but then we move along with our life trying to fix things ourselves.

Moses is God's mouthpiece here. Moses tells the people to fear not, stand firm, and be still (Exod. 14:14–15). Those are three action words which require no action. In other words, God sometimes calls us to do nothing when we face the impossible. Would the Israelites eventually have to step forward and walk through dry land? Yes, but first they had to learn the value of doing nothing.

When we realized our daughter had severe special needs, I wanted to call all of the experts, schedule doctors' appointments, and discuss her case with professionals. I wanted to "fix" her. But there was no fixing it. Three days a week three separate strangers came and provided therapeutic services. My job? Stay silent. It was then I learned how to stand firm. Stand firm in the truth that God would work, and He didn't need my help.

There is beauty in non-action. There is redemption and hope and promise when we sit still and remember God. As we are quiet, and let God work, we often see His hand. When we pray, asking Him for the smallest (or biggest) of requests, we are overjoyed and recognize His loving provision when He shows up. He always shows up! Our smallness, when we sit and be still, reminds us of God's greatness. Psalm 46:10 says, "Be still, and know that I am God." We can remember God is God when we stay still.

As we sit still, we also stand firm in our faith. Faith isn't learned when life is going well; real faith comes when we step back and really let God work behind the scenes, standing firm in the things we know to be true. Believing in those things we cannot see; like how God loves us, provides for us, fights for us, and grows our faith.

God doesn't always fix our situation in the way we want. Instead, God calls us to sit still and wait for His salvation. Sometimes, like with the Hebrews at the Red Sea, we don't have to wait long; but sometimes we have to wait on God for months or even years without getting an answer. God's timing isn't our own, but I know this: God fights for you, even if it's behind the scenes.

So many passages in the Bible call us to be silent and let God work. The apostle Paul knew a little bit about hardships. He faced death, illness, drowning, famine, and injury. In Romans 8:37 (ESV), he says, "No, in all these things we are more than conquerors through him who loved us." How do we conquer the impossible? We stay still, stand firm, and trust that God is at work. We can do this because we understand the depths of God's love for us.

Maybe today your salvation comes in the form of relinquishing. There came a point with my daughter that I had to let God work in her life. I couldn't fix her, but God could. And her healing didn't come in an instant. In fact, it would be two more years before she walked and another four years before she could feed herself. Yet even in that time, God was working—and as I sat still, He brought about growth and healing that couldn't have come if I had been frantically trying to fix everything. Yes, we took her to therapy, consulted doctors, and made a plan. But ultimately God was behind it all.

The path of "nonaction" means we know God is at work, we trust He will fight for us, and we believe God is with us. Just because you can't see His hand doesn't mean He has left you alone. Maybe it is time to let go of trying to change the impossible and allow yourself to rest, be still, and stand firm. Allow God to grow your faith as you face the impossible.

His Presence and Protection

> And the LORD went before them by day in a pillar of cloud to lead the way, and by night in a pillar of fire to give them light . . . and the pillar of cloud went before them and stood behind them. So it came between the camp of the Egyptians and the camp of Israel. (Exod. 13:21; 14:19–20)

When the Israelites left Egypt, God's presence went with them. His presence was in a pillar of cloud during the day and a pillar of fire at night. Exodus 13 says it stayed with them and never left. As the armies of Pharaoh approached the people, Exodus 14:19 says the pillar of God's presence stood before the people and the armies. This presence of God went between them and the evil rushing to consume them.

The enemy would like nothing more than to have us believe these things we didn't sign up for mean that God has left us. As we face the impossible, God often feels incredibly distant, but our emotions do not dictate truth. God had led His people and He had not left them alone. God's presence remained. It is the very thing that protects! Hebrews promises this to all believers:

> For He Himself has said, "I will never leave you nor forsake you." (Heb. 13:5b)

Living in His presence means all of the evil in the world cannot come between me and Him. Yes, evil is real and powerful. The Hebrews faced swords and death. God's promise is not that there will be no hardship, but that no matter what we face, His presence will remain. We have a God who is stronger than our deepest fear and darkest hurt. Living in the presence of God reminds us that His love is unbeatable and unending.

The Israelites had tangible, real, and visible evidence of God's presence! Pillars of cloud and pillars of fire were often used on a smaller scale with armies, who would burn fires and send smoke signals out to communicate with their members. But this was not a man-made phenomenon. Not only was this an awesome view of God's glory, it was practical. When the Pharaoh came to destroy Moses's people, this supernatural presence of God physically kept the Israelites safe as they crossed the Red Sea.

Emboldened by God's presence, the Bible tells us that Moses stepped up while the pillars of cloud and fire defended the Israelites.

> Then Moses stretched out his hand over the sea; and the LORD caused the sea to go back by a strong east wind all that night, and made the sea into dry land, and the waters were divided. (Exod. 14:21)

The Hebrew word for *stretched* means to "spread out" or "cause to yield." In an act of faith and trust with God's visible presence before him, Moses spreads out his arms in surrender and praise to the God who would defend them. While God blew the waters of the Red Sea apart, His presence acted as a defense, and the Israelites were free to walk in safety between the walls of water. Moses and the people crossed over on dry land because the presence of God protected them; and all that was required of them was to yield to Him and trust in His work.

In the middle of life's interruptions, God's presence can still be found. Moses and the Israelites had tangible evidence of God's presence; today, we have access to God's presence through His Word. Our Bibles hold all of the truth, the power, and presence of God we will ever need. Do you want to see God? He is not hidden, as some might say. He is found in the pages of the Bible. Open it and you will see Him there.

A Deeper Faith

> Thus Israel saw the great work which the LORD had done in Egypt; so the people feared the LORD, and believed the LORD and His servant Moses. (Exod. 14:31)

After God's people crossed the Red Sea, Moses stretched out his hands again to vanquish the Pharaoh and his army. The waters rushed together, the Egyptians' wheels got stuck in the mud, and their chariots filled with water. The Pharaoh and his entire army drowned. While the Israelites had walked through on dry land, the waters would not be held back for the Egyptians.

Sometimes God pushes us into the waters of the impossible. Unthinkable things are allowed in our lives, but for a reason. Nothing is wasted with God, and so it is with our suffering. So it is with the twists to our stories. It is all for a purpose—God's purpose.

During Appalachian summers on really hot days, my mom and siblings would pile into the minivan and drive three minutes up the hill behind our house to the local swimming pool. Chlorine and 90's music greeted us as we walked through the entrance. My ten-year-old brother would run to where the deep end was and climb the high ladder to dive into the 12-foot section. I was content swimming in the shallows. Even though I was a good swimmer, the dark blue water frightened me. I didn't like to swim where I couldn't see the bottom.

Sometimes my brother and his friends would sneak up behind me and push me into the deep end. I never found it humorous. Panic creeped into my heart as the water, seeped into my mouth. The first year home with our daughter, I felt like God had pushed me into the deep end of the pool. I longed to be back in shallower water, but God used that deep water experience to grow my faith.

I felt like I was drowning. The rushing water of uncertainty crept up and over into my comfortable life. It was during that time I began reading God's Word daily. I prayed every day for strength. I began living one day at a time. I didn't want to (nor could I) think about the future. So each day I focused on that day. It was all I could handle as I treaded water. I realized that the waters of doubt and worry had the ability to destroy my faith or deepen it. I chose to go deeper. God used that time to increase my faith as I trusted His protection, sought His presence, and believed He would lead me through.

Deeper faith is waiting. It begins with non-action. If you are facing an impossible situation, let me encourage you to stand strong in your faith, don't try to fix it, cry out to God, and wait for Him to move. Often we jump right into fixing our problems, but most of the time, God wants us to wait on Him.

As we pray, read our Bibles, and seek godly counsel, God's presence is there. God has never left us, and we can trust He never will. Recognize that God allows these impossible things in order to grow our faith. He might not part the seas or destroy our enemies, but God will grow our faith.

God's power was demonstrated at the Red Sea. Not just for the Israelites, but for us too. More than three thousand years later we can read the words written by Moses in Exodus to remind our hearts that God still works and is present in our lives. The Israelites' faith in God grew greater that day. We, too, can look at this story to show us that God's great power can grow our faith.

Jesus and Moses

Thunder cracked in the middle of the night. But it wasn't the storm that woke me. I heard a faint cry coming from the bedrooms. I rolled out of bed. Inside the dark room, I heard another whimper and picked up the child. My son cried out my name. He was half awake and drenched in sweat. I calmed the sleepy toddler with gentle rocking motions. The storm outside passed overhead and sleep returned.

The storms of life creep up on us. We awaken from a "normal" life. Wind and destruction rain down. Marriages dissolve. Death steals. Loss happens. Sickness weakens. Grief overwhelms. Is your boat sinking? Are the waves of despair rolling over you? Where is God in all of this?

The disciples of Jesus ran into a storm one night. The rain began to fall and suddenly the light disappeared behind black clouds. The cold air took their breath away. The boat tipped and dove. One wave. Then another. Then another. The circumstances were too much. Have you been there, where you just couldn't catch your breath? Drowning in what seemed like an endless pit of despair?

God has promised to never leave you. Even when doubt threatens to overturn your faith. Those men, who had left their families and jobs to follow Jesus, surely believed He was the Messiah, but doubt crowded their vision.

> But as they sailed He fell asleep. And a windstorm came down on the lake, and they were filling with water, and were in jeopardy. And they came to Him and awoke Him, saying, "Master, Master, we are perishing!"
>
> Then He arose and rebuked the wind and the raging of the water. And they ceased, and there was a calm. But He said to them, "Where is your faith?"

> And they were afraid, and marveled, saying to
> one another, "Who can this be? For He commands
> even the winds and water, and they obey Him!"
> (Luke 8:23–25)

Do not miss the lesson the disciples learned while Jesus was in the boat. Jesus was in control of the storm. All of those circumstances rocking your boat, He holds them. Have faith in Jesus. The One who commands the winds and the waves is still Lord over all. And don't miss the verses right before the storm. Jesus tells them, "Let us cross over to the other side of the lake" (Luke 8:22 CSB).

You might be feeling the rocky waves or the drowning pressure of a life interrupted, but Jesus said to go to the other side. For us we might not know what that looks like, and surely the Israelites didn't know what would be waiting for them on the other side of the Red Sea, but friend we can trust the God who walks with us through the waters. God is ready to demonstrate His power to us to help us see the way to faith.

Sometimes He asks us to step further out and deeper into the storm. We think we've handled all we can handle. And suddenly, we are asked to deal with even more. We had faith while the storm raged around us, but what about when we are asked to do something even scarier? Suddenly we are like Peter, in the middle of something we had no idea was coming (Matt. 14:22–33).

We start sinking because we are focused on the circumstances and not our Savior. Jesus grabs a hold of us. The lesson for Peter (and us) is that Jesus will take hold of us in the storm. Your faith is not up to you. Being brave and casting out fear isn't your job. You don't even have to reach out to Jesus. He's already reaching for you. When the storms of life threaten to overwhelm you, remember Jesus is in control and your faith can be strong because it is rooted in God's goodness and sovereignty.

God's providence that led Moses and the people through the Red Sea is the same providence that is going to lead them to the mountain of God, Mount Sinai. Even though Moses had seen God's amazing power through the burning bush, the ten plagues, and the crossing of the Red Sea, Moses needed to be reminded of God's ability to draw near. It is not enough to have an all-powerful God. We need this God to come down from heaven, even in all of His glory, because in God's glory we see the fullness of God's goodness.

Prayer

O powerful protector God, You were the one who showed up as a pillar of cloud and a pillar of fire for Moses and the children of Israel; may You show up for me today. I have this impossible thing sitting in front of me, and it feels like the Red Sea and there is no way out. I'm scared and I want to fix this. I want to run away or find a solution. You have led me here and You love me, but life is so hard right now. Help me seek Your presence in the Bible and deepen my faith even now. I don't always understand where You are leading me, but I know it is good because You are here. I'll admit I don't have the faith I need, but You promise that nothing is wasted. Please grow my faith in your goodness during this season of facing the impossible. In the midst of even this, You are already good. Amen.

Resting in God's Goodness

What is your first response when you are faced with a hard situation? What do you want to do to fix it?

_____

_____

What do the following verses tell us about being still?

Psalm 46:10

Psalm 62:5

Isaiah 32:17

1 Thessalonians 4:11

Circle which one of these you are struggling with the most:

Standing firm and being strong.

Fearing the situation around me.

Trying to fix the impossible situation myself.

We discover God's presence in the pages of the Bible. Read these verses about God's presence and circle which verse you will hold close to your heart this week.

Exodus 33:14

Psalm 16:11

Acts 3:19

2 Corinthians 3:17

9

The Way to God's Presence

We had finally made it. After years of prayer, countless hours of preparation, lots and lots of tears, selling most of our belongings, and saying goodbye, we arrived in Honduras. The tropical heat hit us like a ton of bricks as my little family of seven stepped out of the plane and walked down the metal steps, walking forward into the great unknown.

Two and half years later God asked us to walk another road again. In one phone call our family's world changed. In one moment, God suddenly removed us from the mission field. We had been discussing several issues with the mission agency we worked under. Over a period of several months, we felt some details needed addressing. We had been open with our agency over some concerns which we thought were minor. Things like job clarification and a breakdown of communication. We wanted things to get better. These were small issues to work through, in our opinion. Instead, the agency took this opportunity to not renew my husband's contract. The expectations of the mission agency and ours suddenly didn't line up. There wasn't a resolution.

The separation did not involve doctrinal nor personal issues. We never disqualified ourselves and our relationship with our fellow missionaries remained intact. It was more of a logistical issue, but we were still hurt by how it was handled. The way we ended up leaving Honduras felt harsh and unnecessarily hard. Our immediate reaction was to feel like God didn't have a plan for us. It was disorienting.

My husband and I had prepared to move to the mission field, but we were not prepared for unexpected changes in our plans. Was God still leading?

After the Red Sea, Moses probably thought the people would go straight to the Promised Land. Instead, God wanted to show him, and the people of Israel, something else.

God's plans for us might include shifts in our stories, but these changes can also lead us to learn more about God and this wonderful truth of drawing near to Him. God interrupted our family's plans to show us who He really is and reveal to us His ability to work in amazing ways.

At the burning bush God called Moses to deliver His people. Following a series of miracles, redemption, and a walk through the water, Moses might have been ready to rest.

Isn't it interesting that God didn't lead Moses and the people straight to the Promised Land? Scholars have said there are many ways the Israelites could have traveled to Canaan. But God had a path for them, even if it didn't look like it made sense on a map. God's map for our lives won't look conventional, but it will be perfect for us. It won't lead us anywhere but to the arms of God if we are willing to stay the course.

My desire to be a missionary started with my mother reading stories of Amy Carmichael and Mary Slessor. I grew up hearing about the Judsons in Burma and Hudson Taylor in China. At the age of twenty I married a man who was willing to go to the mission field, but God didn't lead us there right away. There were medical school loan debts to pay off and God needed to teach us quite a few lessons before we stepped foot on foreign soil. When we arrived in Honduras, I believed I was finally where God wanted me. I was living what my little girl heart had always wanted.

Only it turned out differently. God would take us a different way. He moved us back, and although I don't know how our family will be involved in missions in the future, we know God has called us to missionary work—whether that means to give or to go.

As we see Moses approach the mountain, I believe God had more than just plans to give commandments and instructions. Yes, Moses would write the Ten Commandments and the instructions on how to build the tabernacle. Moses would also leave the mountain with a different view of God. God wanted to show Moses His presence. That was the point.

As we walk through life, are we more concerned with getting to the mountain and seeing the fruit of our waiting and longings? Or are we ready to see God? Are we ready to draw near to God, even if our dreams die? What we have walked through and what God has planned for us in the future might be scary, uncertain, and perplexing. But there are lessons here at the foot of the mountain with Moses.

Do you want to be near to God? God might seem distant and foreign to you today. Let's take a look and see how God's providence teaches us about His presence.

God's Presence Provides

And my God shall supply all your need according
to His riches in glory by Christ Jesus. (Phil. 4:19)

After the victory at the Red Sea, Moses and the people were
ready to rest. God led them from the salty sea water into the wilderness. Moses had lived forty years walking these sands and some
believe he probably knew of an oasis where they could find water.
When they arrived, the water turned out to be bitter (Exod. 15:23).
The people began to complain. There was no food, no water, and
the path was completely uncertain. They blamed Moses and God.

In spite of their grumbling, God turned the bitter water sweet
in Exodus 15:25. It is here we learn another name for God. "Jehovah
Rapha" means "The LORD who heals." The name means to cure or
repair like a physician. They knew God as the all-powerful God who
smote the Egyptians, but they were learning the personal nature of
God. He heals.

It had been about a month since they left Egypt. God wanted
to provide for them, but also test them. After the people came
to Moses to complain, God responded with this in Exodus 16:9:
"Then Moses spoke to Aaron, 'Say to all the congregation of the
children of Israel, 'Come near before the LORD, for He has heard
your complaints.'"

At first, I'll admit my heart complained when God asked us to
move away from Honduras. What we saw as an utter failure and
change of plans turned out to be a testing ground for our hearts.
Would we really trust Him? God also showed up in big ways. Never,

in all of our times in Honduras nor when we returned, did we lack anything. Each day we had everything we needed.

Is there something in your life you think is lacking? A spouse? A better job? A house? Health? Sometimes God allows us to face a time of lacking so we will turn to Him to provide exactly what we need. God used the worldwide shutdown to show our family that He provides for His children. God tells Moses, I'm going to give them exactly what they need. Will they believe His Word? God always wants to reveal Himself as the ultimate provider.

> "Behold, I will rain bread from heaven for you. And the people shall go out and gather a certain quota every day, that I may test them, whether they will walk in My law or not." (Exod. 16:4)

God would provide for them each day, just enough, to test them and to reveal to them that He is a God who provides. God knew what each family needed. It says, "morning by morning" (Exod. 16:21 ESV) they would get up and find what they needed.

One night during the quarantine, I sat the fourth empty bottle of water by the door. In many countries you don't drink the tap water. In fact, you can't brush your teeth or cook using tap water. We had to use "clean" water for anything going inside our bodies. So trucks with 5-gallon bottles of water would drive through our neighborhood selling refills. We had four of those bottles at the time, but after over a week of no water trucks, we were empty.

Before, I would have panicked and made plans to disobey the curfew to go get water; well, I would have sent my husband out to get water. I would have stressed, worried, and probably stayed up for hours in my bed until 2 a.m. thinking, *How will we get water!?* We needed it and all of the worst-case scenarios would have filtered through my mind.

Instead, the two months of isolation had taught me again and again that God would provide. There was no reason to rush and worry. God had shifted my heart to believing Psalm 23 is true. "The LORD is my shepherd; I shall not want." We would never lack.

I praised God that night because I knew we would have water the next day, even though the water trucks usually came on a different day of the week. I went to bed excited to see how God would provide what we needed. How did I know this? Because we needed water and God would provide. I wrote this in my journal the night before:

> "He has never NOT provided. God's provision is a lesson I didn't know I needed to learn. Oh the kindness of God to teach me of His provision during this pandemic. What a good, good Father."

The next day, Monday, the water truck came by. Bright and early before our last gallon was spent. We did not go completely empty because God would never leave us completely dry. So, the Israelites moved through the wilderness, daily eating the bread from heaven the Great Provider gave to them.

The idea of manna and provision were proven throughout the first two months of the pandemic. We had enough food for each day, not much extra. I missed fruits and vegetables, which were hard to find at the grocery store, but one day God sent a man and woman to our neighborhood selling fresh produce. Never was I so happy to see potatoes!

Each time Moses was in need, God stepped in and provided. What do you need today? We can trust Philippians 4:19, "And my God shall supply all your need according to His riches in glory by Christ Jesus." When we are in need, God will supply.

God's Presence Teaches Us

> So the LORD spoke to Moses face to face, as a man speaks to his friend. And he would return to the camp, but his servant Joshua the son of Nun, a young man, did not depart from the tabernacle. (Exod. 33:11)

The people and Moses finally made it to the mountain. Mount Sinai would be the place God would reveal His commandments and renew His covenant with the people. After about three months of travel, Moses and the people set up camp by the mountain. In Exodus 19:3, we read that Moses goes up the mountain. There God reminds Moses it was He who redeemed and protected them (v. 4) and He has plans for them. Part of those plans were to be holy and enter into a covenant with Him (vv. 6–7).

In Exodus 20 we read how God gave Moses the Ten Commandments. How would the people be expected to live with God? How should they live with one another? God told the people what was expected of them. In Exodus 21:1–23:19 God gives instructions to Moses on how to relate to both other people and Himself. God reminds Moses of the promise and the covenant (23:20–23). In Exodus 24–31 God lays out detailed plans on worship. Moses receives instruction on how to build and furnish the tabernacle, which would be the place God would dwell with His people.

In the middle of God speaking to Moses, there was a commotion at the foot of the mountain. Exodus 32 tells us the people built a golden calf to worship. For their idolatry the people were punished. After a time of judgment in which many people died, Moses went back up the mountain. In this exchange between Moses and God we see a change in Moses.

After returning to the mountain, Moses approaches God with a bold request. God had redeemed, provided for, and instructed His people. The next thing for them to do was to enter the Promised Land. Moses stands before God and lays out all of his doubts.

Do we feel close enough with God to be able to lay out our doubts before Him? During our quarantine I began to feel more comfortable with asking God, "why" and "how" and "Are You really there?" So when we moved back to the States, those questions flooded my journal. I poured out my heartache to God on those pages. The first few months of being back I realized something Moses also recognized. We could not move forward without God's presence in our lives.

> Then Moses said to the LORD, "See, You say to me, 'Bring up this people.' But You have not let me know whom You will send with me. Yet You have said, 'I know you by name, and you have also found grace in My sight.' Now therefore, I pray, if I have

found grace in Your sight, show me now Your way, that I may know You and that I may find grace in Your sight. And consider that this nation is Your people." (Exod. 33:12–13)

God tells Moses He will go with them (Exod. 33:14). Then Moses makes a bold request. He says, "Please, show me Your glory" (v. 18). In other words, "Show me who You are, Lord." Moses shifted from "please don't leave me" to "show me Your glory." What would happen in our lives if we shifted our thinking from "God, help!" to "God, show me who You are in this situation."

God's response is amazing and I want to take a closer look at it as we learn what it really means to draw near to God. You see, the mountain wasn't just about laws, rules, and commandments. The mountain was about drawing near to God. All the Israelites knew of God was His power. It was time God invited them into a relationship with Him.

To draw near to God, we must be willing to see God as He is. It is God who draws near to us first. He shows us, tells us, and makes a way for us to be near to Him. If we truly desire to draw near to God, we must first admit this nearness will not be what we expect.

God's Presence Is Our Good

Then He said, "I will make all My goodness pass before you." (Exod. 33:19)

Moses stands before God in Exodus 34 and says, "God, I can't do this." The people had just rebelled against God and built a golden calf. Aaron, Moses's brother, led the way to a great sinful act which caused God to enact judgment on His people He had just delivered. God had great love and great mercy. The people could not continue in their sin. Moses climbs the mountain after dealing with the rebellious Israelites and questions again whether God would really take them to the Promised Land. Moses boldly declares to God, "We aren't going to go unless you go with us" (see Exod. 33:12–13). God says, "I will go with you and give you rest" (see v. 14).

Moses then asks God to show Himself. I can imagine the weariness in Moses. This eighty-year-old man was ready for rest, but God had more for him to do. There was to be more work and more trials. Before stepping into the next part of the journey, God needed to fortify Moses in truth about Himself. God wanted Moses to learn what drawing near to Him really meant.

As I shared in chapter 4, depression wasn't supposed to be part of my story. I didn't sign up for depression. Why was I feeling this way? The bottom of the pit did not provide any answers to my questions.

I remember telling my husband one night, "If I only had a reason to feel this way, it would make it easier." It was the first time in my life I really felt like God had abandoned me. I knew God cared and loved me because the Bible told me so. During the day I would pour into my heart the truth from God's Word, but it all felt empty because the sun would set and night was the worst. The feelings would bubble up and I would cry every night.

God used those weeks, months, and even years battling depression to draw me close to Him. Would I really believe that

God was good? Could I still believe God was good, even when I suffered with feelings of loneliness, sadness, and unexplained grief? Over time my mind shifted as I read a book by Edward T. Welch. In his book *Depression: Looking Up from the Stubborn Darkness*, he says:

> The reason Scripture doesn't give clear guidelines for assigning responsibility is that it is not essential for us to know precise causes. This is good news: you don't have to know the exact cause of suffering in order to find hope and comfort.[7]

We can trust a God who is bigger than our feelings. We can believe in a God who lives beyond our circumstances. He is big enough to not be affected by this sinful world. But He also bends close enough to care for us in a personal way. Moses wanted to see God's glory. God said, "My glory is my goodness" (see Exod. 33:19–23). Want to know what sums up the essence of God? Goodness. Not only that, God makes a statement to Moses in that same exchange that demonstrates His sovereignty. God says, "I will have mercy on whom I will have mercy and compassion on whoever I want" (see Exod. 33:19 ESV).

Do you want to know who He has chosen to impart His mercy? You. Romans 8:1 says there is no condemnation for those who are in Christ. If you are in Christ today, there is no judgment, only mercy. Romans 8:18 goes on to say: "For I consider that the sufferings of this present time are not worthy to be compared with the glory which shall be revealed in us." The suffering we face will reveal God's glory. And that glory? It is good. It is God's presence.

Paul concludes with, "And we know that all things work together for good to those who love God, to those who are the called according to His purpose" (v. 28).

When our eyes turn away from our circumstances and onto God, light can come back into our hearts. The cracks of hope can lead us to the path of hope and comfort. Today you might be experiencing a deep sadness which you can't explain. A loneliness, a grief, a disease, a fear, or something else keeps you from finding comfort and hope.

When the shadows surround us, we are tempted to fear, but God is with us. His presence is good because He is good. Our path might be filled with uncertainty and this doesn't feel good. God says we can find rest because He is both sovereign and good. We have a God who is in control of everything but also a God who loves us so deeply we cannot plunge too far into the depths. Let us sing with Paul these words,

> What then shall we say to these things? If God is for us, who can be against us? . . . For I am persuaded that neither death nor life, nor angels nor principalities nor powers, nor things present nor things to come, nor height nor depth, nor any other created thing, shall be able to separate us from the love of God which is in Christ Jesus our Lord. (Rom. 8:31–39)

> Then he [Moses] said, "If now I have found grace in Your sight, O Lord, let my Lord, I pray, go among us, even though we are a stiff-necked people; and

pardon our iniquity and our sin, and take us as Your inheritance." (Exod. 34:9)

As we walk into the unknown, we need the same thing—God's promised presence. And we have it. God's presence was promised to Moses and God promises to be with us today:

> And we have known and believed the love that God has for us. God is love, and he who abides in love abides in God, and God in him. (1 John 4:16)

> Yea, thought I walk through the valley of the
> shadow of death,
> I will fear no evil;
> For you are with me;
> Your rod and Your staff, they comfort me.
> (Ps. 23:4)

And God promises to dwell with us forever.

> And I heard a loud voice from the throne saying, "Behold, the dwelling place of God is with man. He will dwell with them, and they will be his people, and God himself will be with them as their God." (Rev. 21:3 ESV)

As Moses was used by God to draw the people near, he also showed the people the way to God. It would require sacrifice, blood, and death. Moses was the leader God chose to reveal the path to nearness to God. We are all trying to draw close to God, but we cannot come to Him anyway we wish.

Jesus and Moses

The person of Jesus is actually the presence of God in our lives today. As we have seen before, the name Emmanuel means "God with us." God was planning something way back in the garden of Eden to send His Son to rescue us. He worked through the family of Abraham to build a nation. Moses stood with the people at the foot of Mount Sinai and saw the glory of God's goodness and experienced the cloud and fire of God's presence. God was drawing the people near to Himself.

The presence of God is Jesus. God gave Moses instructions on the mountain for how to approach Him with the tabernacle. It was not arbitrary. God chose the dimensions, the curtains, the candlesticks, the tables, the gold, and the showbread to all point to Jesus. Moses only had shadows of Christ.

The blood that the priests shed for the people would not be enough. The blood of goats and sheep covered the ground of the tabernacle and later the temple for days, weeks, years, decades, and centuries before the One Perfect Sacrifice would cover it all. In one moment Christ took all of our sin and made the last sacrifice. What does this have to do with God's presence? The writer of Hebrews goes on to tell us:

> And having a High Priest [Jesus] over the house of God, let us draw near with a true heart in full assurance of faith, having our hearts sprinkled from an evil conscience and our bodies washed with pure water. Let us hold fast the confession of our hope

without wavering, for He who promised is faithful.
(Heb. 10:21–23)

Friend, we draw near with a true heart in full assurance because Christ has sprinkled His very own blood on our lives so that we may approach the throne of mercy without fear. We have been washed and are now able to hold fast to hope. Not because we are strong but because God, the One who promised, is faithful.

Jesus is why we can draw near. Moses on the mountain brought us a glimpse of God's presence, but with Jesus we see the full picture. Do you want to know what God is like? Look at Jesus. Do you want to experience God's presence in your life, abide in Christ. Be occupied with Christ. Know Him. Study His life. Talk to Him. God's presence is not a mystery like it was for Moses. God's presence is living inside of us.

For the law of the Spirit of life in Christ Jesus has made me free from the law of sin and death. (Rom. 8:2)

The work of the Spirit in our lives allows us, even when life is interrupted, to start living a life of faith and obedience. As Moses stood on the mountain and stood before the people to recite the laws, he demonstrated to us our next steps. More than anything, when our stories shift, we want to know "what's next?" The next step we take is obedience.

Prayer

Dear God of the mountain, meet me here in the valley. My heart feels heavy with fear of the future and I long to feel close to You. I pray that You will hold me close to You. Let me put my trust today in the blood of Jesus Christ. I hold fast to the truth that You are faithful, even when I am not. Help me to hope today, even though I can't see the way. I hope and trust in the goodness that is Your presence. Be near to me, as You promised, and give me the comfort only You can. Amen.

Resting in God's Goodness

When was the last time you felt really close to God?

_____

_____

_____

What keeps you from approaching God? Is it sin? Fear? Shame? Guilt?

_____

_____

_____

How does understanding the goodness of God change the way you see God's presence in your life?

_____

_____

_____

Read through these verses on God's presence. What additional truths do you find about God's presence in them?

Psalm 139:7

Psalm 95:2

Ephesians 3:12

Hebrews 10:19

James 4:10

What can you change about your daily routine in order to experience God's presence?

_____

_____

_____

10

Obedience and Faith

After being in Honduras for over a year and half, we hosted our second surgical team. The team members flew down on a Friday. My husband used the church's buses to pick up the people and their luggage. Not to mention all the medications needed for the following week's surgical clinic. I imagined the smiles, laughter, joy, and exhaustion etched on their faces. I say imagine because I wasn't there to greet the team of doctors, nurses, and surgical technicians. They had traveled to Honduras to perform surgeries from Monday-Thursday. They would change the lives of people living in pain. Hernias, gallbladders, and a few other minor procedures were on the list. The surgeries would be minor, but the change could be eternal. Each patient would also be given the gospel message over the course of several weeks.

That evening when they arrived, I piled our five children into our car and drove across the road to the surgical center. My husband had dropped off the team earlier that afternoon. Now it was time for dinner. I had prepared a meal. As I sat around the table learning the names and faces of the people who would serve with my husband that week, I inwardly felt out of place.

As a mother of five children, I live in a constant state of distraction. My life is filled with children's voices, playing board games, watching silly YouTube videos, and breaking up sibling disagreements. As the nurses and doctors talked about the surgical cases, traveling, and what would come in the next few days, my heart was a little jealous.

There would be ladies from our church helping with registration, taking vitals, and checking patients in. There would be people grabbing supplies and helping to make the patients comfortable before and after surgery. That first night the team arrived I realized I was not going to be a part of this. We had left friends and family, endured a global pandemic, and my entire life was turned upside down, but for what? So, I could watch children?

That evening I packed up my crew and left my husband to talk to the team. It was then, after putting the kids to bed, I felt my insignificance. When Monday rolled around and surgeries started, I could feel the excitement in my husband's demeanor and attitude. Inwardly I was sad. It wasn't the first time I had felt this, but suddenly I was face-to-face with how my own faith and obedience look very different from my husband's. I would not be with patients. I would not be with the visiting team members.

During that week in July, I prayed for each patient and the team members. As problems arose, I prayed with my husband as he worked to solve the issues. We prayed for salvation. We prayed for healing. But in my praying I felt feeble. I wanted to ask God, "How can I serve You better than just praying. Why I am stuck here babysitting?"

No one sees the work behind the scenes. Maybe no one notices your work right now. Do you care for an elderly parent? Or a special needs child? Do you teach kids who are not your own every day? Maybe you are just tired of a job you don't like. Maybe you do your job and never hear "thank you." Life is filled with unseen work. Working for days, weeks, months, and years doing the hidden work that no one sees can grow a seed of bitterness.

God has called me into a life of invisible work because this is what obedience looks like. Obedience is not often shiny or pretty. Obeying God is sometimes about being behind the scenes instead of out on stage. This is why obedience cannot exist without faith. James talks about this in the New Testament. He says that faith without obedience (or works) is not possible (James 2:14–19). Together faith and obedience work side by side.

Over the years, as much as my work has been invisible, I've seen obedience as an act of faith. One does not follow the other. We need both, working together like two strands of a rope. Serving and working for God means we serve with faith and obedience.

What did Moses believe and trust about God? What did Moses do because of his beliefs? If we are going to find contentment in doing the unseen work, we don't need to find a stage, we need to stay steady in our faith.

As we look at the life of Moses, from the burning bush to the mountain and beyond, we see faith and obedience. Moses was the leader, the face, and the deliverer in the eyes of the people of Israel. But to God, and for Moses, his life was filled with simple obedience and practical faith.

When we last left Moses, he was on the mountain developing a friendship and closeness with the Lord, Yahweh. God called Moses to the mountain for a reason. Not just to reveal His goodness and sovereignty, but to tell Moses how to serve and worship Him. In the books of Exodus, Leviticus, and Deuteronomy we find the instructions God revealed to Moses. Laws, sacrifices, building plans, and more were written down and recorded. Moses spoke the words to the Israelites. He wrote the words down for them. Spent hours writing and speaking to the people. Even more hours were spent with God learning His ways. Within these books we see how Moses's faith and obedience played out.

Instead of walking through every single detail of Moses's life as he received the law, we are going to look at a few passages that show how Moses's faith was demonstrated in his obedience. How can we move forward, even when life doesn't go as planned, with faith and obedience? Moses believed things about God, things he learned from God in the desert, from the ten plagues, the Red Sea, and at the mountain. All of those truths would keep Moses going, even when he didn't see a clear path.

Entering motherhood was complicated and messy, and it was humbling as I realized most of my work for the Lord God would go unseen by the world. God transitioned me into a season of unexpected loneliness and depression those first few months as a new mother. In the moving and shifting I realized faith had to be my foundation. Obedience would become a choice I made each day.

The obedience of taking care of my family, especially when no one was looking, was going to be the key to surviving this change. Moses was moving from deliverer to leader. He no longer would be rescuing the people. He would be leading the people. But how? What would enable him to lead? Faith.

Friend, if you find yourself in a season of unexpected hardship with shifting sands of uncertainty, hang on to faith. If your foundation of faith is wobbly, spend this season to build a stronger foundation. Our God who walks with us today is the same God who met Moses on the mountain. He is the same sovereign and good God who asks us to walk by faith, not by sight.

We can't always understand why God allows things to happen to us, but we can trust God will strengthen our faith and lead us toward obedience no matter the future. Moses didn't know the future. He didn't know the future of the Israelites nor if they would really make it to the Promised Land.

The land of Canaan, promised by God to them, was not empty. There were people and nations they would have to drive out and conquer. Moses probably thought of this because we saw in the last chapter that he asked God to go with them. He knew they would need God. We need God too.

God's presence would go with them. God would empower them. God would fight for them. You and I can rest in these truths as well. Not a type of resting that involves non-action. We aren't talking about sitting on the couch waiting for God to move. We need to rest with confidence to keep moving forward in obedience. What does that look like? How do we find the faith and obedience we need to resist the despair that comes with our stories shifting? Moses's story reveals this in Leviticus.

Faith Begins with Hearing

Now the LORD called to Moses, and spoke to him
from the tabernacle of meeting, saying . . . (Lev. 1:1)

It all begins with Moses hearing God's voice and God's laws. First, God tells Moses how to build the tabernacle of meeting. This word *tabernacle* means house or dwelling place. This is a place God describes at the end of Exodus. It would be built to house God's presence (Exod. 36).

Some translations read, "Tent of meeting," or "tabernacle of the congregation" (Lev. 1:1). The actual Hebrew meaning for this word is "abiding, dwelling place, or covering." This was a tent-like structure the people carried with them to use while traveling to the Promised Land. God gave Moses detailed instructions on how to build it. Moses met with God in the tabernacle. Not only that, he would hear God speak from the tabernacle. God's presence was said to fill the tabernacle every time Moses went to speak to God.

The entire book of Leviticus is a record of what God spoke to Moses. Then what Moses spoke to the children of Israel. What did God tell Moses? The Law. In the New Testament, when you find Moses's name, it is almost always associated with the phrase, the "Law of Moses." What laws are we referring to?

The laws are about sacrifices, worship, sin, and praise. God would use this time in Moses's life to explain how life worked. Leviticus is a hard book to read, but if we understand the heart and message behind it, we see the beauty of obedience and faith. How should people approach God? How should people interact with each other? God showed them in the book of Leviticus.

If the Ten Commandments are the foundation for God's law, Leviticus gives us details into what this particularly looked like for the ancient Hebrews. We might be tempted to look at those lists and think they don't apply to us. Second Timothy 3:15–16 reminds us that "all Scripture" is there for our benefit. Even Leviticus.

One of the phrases that is repeated over and over again is this idea of God speaking to Moses and then Moses speaking to the children of Israel. How are we to move forward in our faith? By listening. Moses does a lot of listening in the book of Leviticus. Faith and obedience begin with listening. For us, we don't hear the audible words of God, but we do have His Word written down for us in the Bible.

One day after a particular hard night as a mother, I remember calling my own mother. My toddler had gotten up early that day and my newborn had been up all night. I was at the point of delirium. I remember crying to my mom on the phone. I said something like, "What am I doing with my life?" Although I don't remember her exact words, I remember her telling me to try to get them both to lay down at the same time in the afternoon. If I did that one thing each day, I would be able to get some rest as well. That became my goal each day. Both my boys would nap at the same time so I could close my eyes and rest as well. Or have some time to sit in the quiet. I might even read a little. It made for better evenings and a happier Mom for sure.

I listened to the voice of my mother because she had been exactly where I was. She knew what it was like to raise children. Her wisdom came from experience. I would have never heard this advice if I hadn't called her. It seems silly to say that because it's so simple. But if we want to hear God's voice, we have to go to the Bible. That's where He has spoken.

Second Peter 1:2–3 says, "Grace and peace be multiplied to you in the knowledge of God and of Jesus our Lord, as His divine power has given to us all things that pertain to life and godliness."

Through the Bible you already have all you need to obey. Do we understand everything in the Bible? Not quite. Can we learn what we need to learn? Absolutely! Moses could not have understood all that God was teaching him at first. Just a quick glance into Leviticus and we also might get confused with the burnt offerings and sacrifices. Even in Moses's limited understanding, he strove to obey. So can we.

Obedience Is Success

> "See, I have set before you today life and good, death and evil, in that I command you today to love the LORD your God, to walk in His ways, and to keep His commandments, His statutes, and His judgments, that you may live and multiply; and the LORD your God will bless you in the land which you go to possess." (Deut. 30:15–16)

God does not require us to understand everything, but He has spoken enough truth for us to know what to do today. At the end of all of the commandments, Moses speaks his final words to the people of Israel in the book of Deuteronomy. One of the things he says to them in the very last section is about obedience (see Deut. 30:1–3). "You know what you need to do." The Israelites had a detailed outline of how to worship and obey God.

We've established that complete understanding of the ins and outs of God's commands are not necessary for simple obedience. However, we might struggle with how God wants us to move forward. What does obedience look like, practically speaking?

During our first few years on the mission field, my husband and I struggled with displaced plans, interrupted dreams, and an uncertain future. COVID shifted our plans, but it also caused us to think about what true success looked like. After a few teams had to be canceled, my husband struggled with feelings of failure. If his job was to host teams from the United States and that wasn't happening, was he being successful?

When we returned home, we continued to ask ourselves, "Was this work we did in Honduras successful?"

As we wrestled with this idea, we concluded that obedience is success. We were obedient to God. Of course, we sinned as humans, but overall we did what God had asked us to do. It feels hard to believe we are living right now in success even though we had to leave. How do we move forward when we've messed up or nothing is going as we imagined?

Moses's life, as we will discover, did not end with him living in the Promised Land. God was not finished interrupting Moses's plans. So what made Moses a success? His obedience. Obedience to what he knew to be true.

What do you know to be true? Read the Bible. Go to church. Listen to podcasts and listen to good preaching, attend a Bible study, or simply devote time once a week to dive into a passage of

Scripture. You don't need a Bible degree to study and understand the Bible. God will meet you and teach you and guide you in His Word. He promises to do so. When we find ourselves unable to see into the future because our plans are cloudy, we can trust that there are things right now God is asking us to do.

Moses continued to listen to God.

Moses continued to meet with God.

Moses continued to teach the people.

Moses was not idle.

In Leviticus, Numbers, and Deuteronomy we read how Moses would hear a word from the Lord and immediately take action. When God instructed him to offer burnt offerings, he did it. Notice the idea of "when" and not "if." I did not say, "If God told Moses . . ." but "When God told Moses . . ." God does not give us ambiguity when it comes to commands. There are things in the Bible that are more principles than commands, but the commands are clear.

So many people want to know what God's will is for their lives. Or they struggle to know what God is calling them to do. Friend, God calls all of us to one thing: obey His commands (1 John 3:24). If you still don't know what that is, go to the Word. God's Word is clear on what is right and pure.

The Hidden Work of Obedience

> Therefore we also, since we are surrounded by so great a cloud of witnesses, let us lay aside every weight, and the sin which so easily ensnares us, and let us run with endurance the race that is set before us, looking unto Jesus, the author and finisher of our faith, who for the joy that was set before Him endured the cross, despising the shame, and has sat down at the right hand of the throne of God. (Heb. 12:1–2)

So, what's the next step? For me and my husband, obeying God means seeking to be involved in missions by going on short-term trips. Praying about serving on a different field. Wisely researching other organizations to be involved in. We also attend church weekly and are involved in serving our community here in West Virginia. My husband ministers to coworkers and patients at the hospital. I am teaching and hosting a Bible study in my home.

There will be small acts of obedience in our lives that no one but God will ever see. Does that mean they don't matter? No. Every time you send a kind note, make a meal, write a text, or pray for someone, God sees. If you are weary and empty today because life just isn't going as you planned, take heart. Believe me when I say God sees you. God sees every single act of faith and obedience.

It takes us a few moments to read through all of the laws and instructions in Leviticus, but those words represent days, weeks, and months of Moses meeting with God. Each and every day Moses would get up and go to the tent of meeting. He would stand or sit and write out everything God said. We will look more deeply into Psalm 90–91 later, but I want to pull out a familiar verse we might have all heard before and that talks about this idea of a hidden season: "He who dwells in the secret place of the Most High shall abide under the shadow of the Almighty" (Ps. 91:1).

When I read about those "secret" places, I think of my friend. My mother used to babysit this friend and her sister when they were little. They would spend their summer days at our house. We would play Barbies and paper dolls. Remember the cut-out paper dolls? Hours were spent outside swimming in a small pool on the patio or swinging on the swing set.

One night I got to go home with her to have a sleepover. It was the best thing ever for a nine-year-old. My friend only had one sister, and they had separate rooms. I shared a room with my two sisters. She also had a huge basement full of toys and secrets. I'll never forget the first night she showed me her "secret place." It was under a stairwell and filled with blankets, pillows, and a small light bulb to illuminate the hideaway. We giggled and laughed until late into the night, hidden away.

For so long I thought God's secret place was a place to look for, but instead I found it is a place I already live in. Where does God have you? Running errands for ailing parents? Waiting in waiting rooms for news? Standing by the phone for that call? Up all night with fussy babies? Thinking about your teenager or adult child?

Today, I want you to know God sees you. Sitting with your coffee, tea, or Diet Coke, you may feel like your days and hours are hidden places. But most of life, and many moments of obedience, are done in hidden places.

Jesus and Moses

Jesus lived in the hidden places. Yes, our Savior had a public ministry, but many moments were not recorded in the Gospels. What about the moments on the mountain when Jesus would sneak off and pray? No one knows the prayers He prayed there.

Jesus was the Almighty Savior, unchangeable and omnipresent. In Him we see the fullness of God (Col. 1:15–20). Yet Jesus limited Himself. Not because He had to, but because He wanted to. Jesus chose to keep His ministry small. The One who had created each and every person limited His influence to twelve apostles. Jesus lived and worked in a small part of the world. His ministry wasn't televised or broadcasted.

There were no live streaming videos of His sermons nor did the whole world see firsthand the miracles performed on those who were blessed with healing. There was no social media to share the good news of Jesus's coming. Jesus moved and served in small, rural towns in the middle of an occupied Israel. Jesus didn't even travel the entire Promised Land. He focused all of His efforts within a small geographical space.

Jesus's obedience would eventually lead Him to the cross. In Jesus's obedience we see a reflection of Moses's as well. We might even say Moses was more famous than Jesus during His time on earth. But Moses (and Jesus) did not obey to be famous nor did they obey so others would see.

Part of faithful obedience is about doing the things we know we are to do, without being seen. If you are feeling hidden, unseen, or suddenly unimportant, remember we are not called to a life on a platform. We are called to live a life pleasing God. Our friend Moses and our Lord Jesus walked in both faith and obedience, not for the sake of their own glory, but for the glory of God.

If your quiet work for God feels like a failure, count yourself faithful instead. For you are reflecting the Christ who came before and Moses who also walked a faithful obedient life. There is work to do—even when no one notices. Other than imparting the laws to the people, Moses also served the people through intercession. Pleading with God on behalf of the people was something Moses did over and over again. As we will see in the next chapter, God can often use those interrupted times in our lives to minister to others through the power of prayer and intercession.

Prayer

Dear heavenly Father who sees me right here, I feel lost and forgotten today. No one else sees all of the hard work I do every day. No one acknowledges or says "thank you." I feel like if I disappeared, no one would notice. But You notice me. You see me. You have placed me here in this life to know You more and serve You right where I am. I surrender my desires. Speak to my heart today through Your Word. Remind me that You have not forgotten me and You never will! Amen.

Resting in God's Goodness

What is one job you do every day that no one else notices?

_____

_____

_____

How does knowing God sees your faithfulness make you feel?

_____

_____

_____

What kind of service to God has been placed on your heart to do for God?

_____

_____

_____

How does understanding the goodness of God change the way you see your seasons where you feel unseen?

_____

_____

_____

Read through the following verses about how God sees us. What additional truths do you find about God's love for us in them?

Proverbs 15:3

Psalm 33:18

2 Chronicles 16:9

Read Isaiah 49:14–16. How do these verses encourage your heart to believe that God will never forget you?

_____

_____

_____

11

Spies and Sons

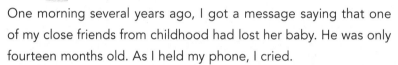

One morning several years ago, I got a message saying that one of my close friends from childhood had lost her baby. He was only fourteen months old. As I held my phone, I cried.

In those early morning hours, I remember deciding in my heart to walk into this grief with my friend. It was not my grief. It wasn't my child. It wasn't my sadness and it didn't need to touch me, but none of us can escape loss. So, I wrapped my heart around my friend's grief and cried all of the tears.

We met at a coffee shop. As I walked in, she stood up from the table and we embraced, weeping with each other. She had tasted the bitterness of loss and I wrapped her grief around me. I could honestly say I was weeping with someone who was weeping.

When life is interrupted and the future holds nothing but confusion, we need someone to pray the prayers we need, taking our burdens to the Throne of Mercy. As our world shatters, we can seek out others who are hurting and learn to cry with them. We can also turn to Christ. Our great Intercessor stands between us and the future. Moses was intercessor for the children of Israel. He stood before God on many occasions and prayed for the people. Jesus is this Man for us.

Taking on my friend's grief meant that even today I still have his birthday saved on my calendar. Each year I send her a text, wishing him a happy birthday. I say his name. I whisper prayers for her whenever the Lord nudges my heart. In September I always remember that horrible feeling of grief and let her know that she is not alone in her weeping. It has been several years since his death, but it changed me. That whole experience has made me more aware of what it really means to intercede for people. More than that, it pointed me to the truth of Christ's intercession.

The dictionary defines *intercede* as, "to interpose on behalf of someone in difficulty or trouble, as by pleading or petition."[8] The Bible takes this idea of acting or helping to explain how Jesus intercedes for us. The *Easton's Bible Dictionary* describes Christ's intercession as this: "He pleads for and obtains the fulfillment of all the promises of the everlasting covenant. . . . He can be 'touched with the feeling of our infirmities,' and is both a merciful and a faithful high priest. . . . Through him we have 'access' to the Father."[9]

One of the most humbling aspects of Moses was his willingness to intercede for the people. There are three separate events that take place in the book of Numbers that teach us what biblical intercession looks like. After looking at these stories of Moses, Aaron, and the people of Israel, we will see how the stories give us actionable steps to take for when we want to intercede for the people in our lives.

Spies

"Pardon the iniquity of this people, I pray, according to the greatness of Your mercy, just as You have forgiven this people, from Egypt even until now." (Num. 14:19)

After the people received the Law of Moses from God, they were instructed in how to build the tabernacle. God would dwell with His people, and this unique tent-like structure would be able to go with them all the way on their journey to the Promised Land. After leaving Mount Sinai they traveled by foot. If they took a direct route, they would have come to Canaan, the Promised Land, in just eleven days. Instead, God took them around a different path.

After several months, the people stood at the edge of God's promise for them. How did they feel? How did Moses feel? Maybe he felt like his job was over. They were here. Before entering the land, they sent in twelve spies, one for each of the twelve tribes of Israel. When the spies returned, they gave a report. Ten of the spies gave a bad report.

And they gave the children of Israel a bad report of the land which they had spied out, saying, "The land through which we have gone as spies is a land that devours its inhabitants, and all the people whom we saw in it are men of great stature. There we saw the giants (the descendants of Anak came from the giants); and we were like grasshoppers

in our own sight, and so we were in their sight."
(Num. 13:32–33)

The majority of the people's response revealed their lack of faith. They "wept" (Num. 14:1) with sorrow because they felt as if all hope was lost. They cried all night long until their sadness turned to anger. The word for *murmured* (Num. 14:2 KJV) here means to grumble and complain. The people's answer to the problem of these "giants" was to give up and go back to Egypt. Even after the plagues, the Red Sea, the water and food in the desert, and the thunderings from the mountain, God's people doubted.

Moses and Aaron tried to reason with them. Then Joshua and Caleb, two of the twelve spies, stood with Moses and encouraged the people to have faith. The people were insistent. They took up stones to kill Moses, Aaron, Joshua, and Caleb. In that instant, God's glory appeared. Out of what many scholars believe was the pillar of cloud, God spoke. Numbers 14:11–12 says that God was ready right then to destroy the people once and for all.

In Numbers 14:13–19 Moses recorded his prayer for the people. This was a prayer of desperation. Moses pleaded for the people by first appealing to God's reputation. Moses reminds God, not because God had forgotten, but because Moses and the people needed to remember God's amazing power, love, and promises. Moses basically says, "What will the other nations think? You have brought these people out of slavery to only destroy them in the desert?"

Then Moses mentions God's loving-kindness and mercy. Numbers 14:17–18 says, "And now, I pray, let the power of my Lord be great, just as You have spoken, saying, 'The LORD is longsuffering and abundant in mercy, forgiving iniquity and transgression."

Moses begged for mercy not because God was obligated to give it, but because God's character is wrapped up in His abundant mercy. Moses reminded himself and the people that God is filled with justice and mercy. Like all of us, we deserve the punishment of eternal damnation, but God is "rich in mercy" (Eph. 2:4).

Many have tried to understand how God can be completely just while also being completely merciful. Christ is the answer. Jesus completely satisfied God's wrath on the cross so that the forgiveness, mercy, and long-suffering is ours to receive.

Moses stood between the people and God's wrath just as Jesus Himself stood before God and us on the cross. Today Jesus stands between God and us, interceding for us (Rom. 8:34). Unlike Jesus, Moses did not have to take on God's complete wrath to save the people in Numbers 14, but Moses's prayer reminds us that we can plead to God for others.

Do we pray for those who are caught up in their sin? The coworker? The neighbor? The family member? Those people who treat you poorly may need salvation. Jesus commanded we pray for everyone:

> "But I say to you, love your enemies, bless those who curse you, do good to those who hate you, and pray for those who spitefully use you and persecute you." (Matt. 5:44)

No one is exempt from deserving God's justice against sin. No one is righteous (Rom. 3:10), no one understands or seeks God

(v. 11), and no one does anything good (v. 12). Our souls, minds, hearts, and actions are naturally sinful. Nothing about our natural state could even hold a spark of hope or goodness.

Our sin is all consuming and the punishment is death (v. 23). The gospel, or "good news" begins with sin because we must be willing to look at where we really stand before God. We truly need the bad news first. We are all sinners deserving the wrath and judgment of God. Our righteousness or good works amount to nothing. There is no boasting at the foot of the cross. The worst thing about us is actually the best news because our sinful state is not the end of the story.

Realizing we are deeply corrupted by sin and have no hope of saving ourselves means we are ready to look up. According to the gospel, being at the bottom is actually the best place we could be because now we are ready to see that God reaches down into the pit of sin and offers salvation.

It is in the pit of rebellion we look to Christ, our great Intercessor who has paid the price to stay God's wrath. In Christ's example we lift up those in prayer who are still in danger. We don't need to be preachers or missionaries to share the gospel. Just as Moses interceded in prayer for the people in Numbers 14:13–19, we too can intercede for those who are on the path to experience God's wrath. God forgave the people in Numbers 14:20, "Then the Lord said: 'I have pardoned, according to your word.'" Pray for those who need God's forgiveness!

Sons

And he stood between the dead and the living; so
the plague was stopped. (Num. 16:48)

The next time Moses and his brother Aaron intervene for the
people is in Numbers 16. It says in verses 1–2 that a man named
Korah rose up against Moses. He stood up and challenged Moses's
authority and actions. These men were chosen as special men to
serve before God in worship. In verse 3 it says, "for all the congregation is holy." In an act of rebellion, they claimed their actions
were holy. How often do we rise up in "holy anger" unaware of our
own sinful hearts?

The sons of Korah in this chapter were relatives of Levi, so
probably Moses and Aaron's cousins. Not only did they oppose
Moses, they did so in a bold and public way. They gathered 250
other "princes," or leaders of Israel, to demand Moses make God
accessible for everyone. In other words, the men were asking to
approach God without a mediator. Throughout Scripture, God has
revealed the truth that men need a mediator. In Genesis 3:15 God
says that there would always have to be someone to act as a go-
between because of sin.

In our sin we need someone to bridge the gap between us
and God. Once again Jesus Christ is that mediator. In the New
Testament the authors pointed back to the work of Christ. In the
Old Testament every story, every event, and every record of history
points to the coming work of Christ. As we saw in Exodus, God
had set up a system in which God's people would approach God.
It would be through the mediator of Moses and later the priests.

The first thing Moses did in Numbers 16 was fall on his face in humility and then immediately turned the matter over to God. Numbers 16:4–5 says, "So when Moses heard it, he fell on his face; and he spoke to Korah and all his company, saying, 'Tomorrow morning the LORD will show who is His and who is holy, and will cause him to come near to Him. That one whom He chooses He will cause to come near to Him.'"

There would be a contest. The people needed to see which men God would recognize as walking in truth. Would it be Moses and Aaron or the sons of Korah? Each of these men would take fire, incense, and coals. They would come to the door of the tabernacle. As they did so, they would be coming near to the presence of God.

It is interesting to note that these men were probably part of the congregation called by God in Numbers 8:19 to serve in the temple. They were already a part of the Levitical priestly family, but they wanted more. In their anger against Moses and Aaron, they rose up in rebellion. They believed they should enter the Promised Land, even though God had commanded them not to. They wanted to go and conquer the land on their own. Moses and Aaron said no.

What do you do when people are against you? I admit I get angry and I like to complain to others who I know will be on my side. Moses didn't turn to Aaron or his wife, Moses turned to God with his frustration. In Numbers 16:15 it says, "Then Moses was very angry, and said to the LORD . . ." Moses's anger, whether sinful or not, was not directed to the Lord, but he definitely took his frustrations to God. When our hearts are angry about how our life feels interrupted, maybe because of other people's choices, we are tempted to complain to everyone but God.

The first thing I do when other people are making bad choices that affect me is text two people. One of them is my sister and the other is my mom. I know both will be on my side. When life hands me something hard, I am so guilty of telling those around me first before lifting up a prayer to God. Have you ever run to a friend or family member upon hearing bad news? Moses turned his heart directly to God.

In the end God pronounced judgment on Korah and recognized Moses as the true leader. Numbers 16:23–24 says that God told Moses to warn the people to get away from the tents of these men: Korah, Dathan, and Abiram. Even in God's wrath, God is merciful. Some ran away from the tents, but others stood by the rebellious men. In this passage we see God gives man a choice to run away from sin or to be swallowed up by the coming judgment.

The earth itself opened up in a miraculous way and swallowed the men's tents and their families. As we see in the passage, not all of the rebellious men were near their tents when their families were destroyed. Some were still near the tabernacle. God sent a fire (Num. 16:35) to consume the rest of these men and all those who were standing with them.

Throughout this entire story, Moses did not stand off and watch God's judgment on these men. Even though they had spoken against him, Moses stayed to warn them. From Moses's position, he did not have to warn the people about the coming judgment, but he did. Do we speak up to warn others about the coming judgment?

After this incident, there arose among the people of Israel a group that began to complain. They blamed Moses for the deaths of their friends and family. God once again stands up for Moses and says, "Get away from among this congregation, that I may consume them in a moment" (Num. 16:45). A plague, some sort of physical ailment that killed people right away, had already started to spread throughout the camp of Israel. Once again, because of their sinful hearts God's wrath was unleashed on the people. Notice, it is not God's wrath that begins this plague, it is the sinfulness of the people's hearts and words. Sin always comes before God's wrath.

In the next few verses we see a beautiful picture of Christ. Moses tells Aaron to use an incense to "make atonement for the people." Numbers 16:48 says, "And he stood between the dead and the living; so the plague was stopped." Can you see Christ today, standing between the dead and the living holding up the proof of atonement?

Before God's throne in heaven Christ holds up His very blood as proof of our atonement. God accepts the atonement in Numbers 16 and the plague stops. So, it is for those plagued with sin who come to Christ. It is not in the coming we are saved; it is in the coming to Christ. The people were not able to come to Moses and Aaron. So, Aaron runs into the middle of death to save those who didn't deserve it.

Our sin is deep, destructive, and deserving of the righteous and holy wrath of God. If we would remember how dark our sin truly is we would see this event as compassionate. They all (us included) deserve God's wrath because of sin. When Aaron provides atonement for the people, this should make us weep with joy at the thought of Christ running into the midst of our sin and holding up his blood-stained hands as proof of our atonement. The people had no way to come to Aaron for cleansing, but Aaron ran straight into the midst of death to save those still alive.

Christian, we were not saved in our coming to Christ, we are saved because Christ came to us. Before we were saved, we all used to walk willingly and purposefully toward hell. Our sin placed us on this path, but God in His goodness and sovereignty has plucked you and me out of this line of sinners to sit with Him. Today we sing with Paul in Romans 8:1 (ESV), "There is therefore now no condemnation for those who are in Christ." We were like the sons of Korah, sons of sinful flesh, but God has made us sons of light to sit with the true Son, Jesus Christ.

When that voice in your head says, "I didn't sign up for this . . ." it is easy to turn inward. Moses experienced some suddenly unplanned moments in his leading the people to the Promised Land. Instead of feeling sorry for himself or angry at those around him, Moses turned to God. Then he sought to intercede for the people.

As we walk forward, believing God's promises and seeing God's power, and trusting God's presence, we can see that our purpose goes beyond a relationship with God. As we walk this journey of life, we will come across people who need prayer. Moses teaches us this great truth that we can pray for others! As our story shifts our eyes shift from our own stories to those around us. We can see with the eyes of Christ. You and I can turn our gaze outward to those who might need us to intercede for them.

In the intercession we find purpose. My family has experienced great loss, great disappointment, and severe sorrow from decisions other people have made. It would be easy to rise up in holy anger. It is much harder, but sweeter in the end, to sing like David:

> Do not keep silent,
> O God of my praise!
> For the mouth of the wicked and the mouth of
>   the deceitful
> Have opened against me;
> They have spoken against me with a lying tongue.
> They have also surrounded me with words of
>   hatred,
> And fought against me without a cause.
> In return for my love they are my accusers,
> But I give myself to prayer. (Ps. 109:1–4)

Notice the author of Psalm 109 tells God, "This is not fair! Do you see what they are doing!?" Then, the last phrase says, "But I give myself to prayer." Give yourself to prayer, friend. Pray for those who speak ill of you. Pray for those in the path of God's wrath. Lift up your hands in prayer to the Father who loves you and Jesus who sees you.

Jesus and Moses

Through these events we see Jesus in the life of Moses. Moses provides for us a picture of the work of Jesus Christ. Moses's life and these events might have happened thousands of years ago, but Jesus lives to intercede for us today (Heb. 7:25).

Moses's life was an ever-shifting story, yet he stepped up, over and over again, to encourage the people. Do we see the shifts in our stories as opportunities to build up those around us? Jesus Christ spent His entire life modeling this type of intercession for us. As Moses's life unfolds in these three events, we see Moses reveal to us these three ways Christ intercedes for us.

In Numbers 14, 16, and 21 we read how the people needed intercession because of their complaining, pride, rebellion, and distrust in God. Moses had to listen to those complaints and doubts because he was God's leader and mediator for the people. God used each account to remind the people that they were really upset at God, not Moses. When people mistreat us, we must remember it comes from a sinful heart that is naturally bent on rejecting God. There is no one who does good. So when people disappoint us, we need not be surprised or worried. God has our backs.

Jesus has our backs as well. Not only is Jesus a better Moses (Heb. 1:3–6), Jesus is the perfect Mediator. He knows our sorrows, even the secret ones. He sees our disappointments and heartaches. He also sees the wrong that has been done to us. He sees and He will make it right.

Moses was counted as faithful in all His house (Heb. 3:5), meaning the tabernacle. Moses was faithful to work as a mediator between God and the people for many years. The author of Hebrews brings up Moses in Hebrews 3 to make the emphasis that even though Moses faithfully led the people all those years, Jesus is even more faithful than Moses. According to Hebrews, Moses was there to point us to Christ.

This is meant to give us hope and encouragement to stand firm until the end. Your life will always hold winding roads filled with uncertainty, but our faith and foundation is in Christ. He will remain faithful, and even when we struggle, Jesus is faithful—even more faithful than Moses.

Our Intercessor also asks us to intercede for others, even when our life feels upside down. Being obedient, praying for others, and serving God faithfully marked Moses's life, and those things can characterize our lives as well. You might feel like in this season you have nothing to offer. You do. God has a job for you. Not only that, God's plan for your life is not over.

What feels like the death of a dream, a plan, a life you loved, can be just the beginning and it can be a season of great growth. How? In the remembering. As we close out Moses's life, we have some of his last words to the people in the book of Deuteronomy and Psalm 90. Let's take a look at what Moses wanted to tell the people, and us, about God.

Prayer

Dear Jesus, our great Mediator, may You be close to me today. I feel the ache of disappointment, even from people I once trusted. I pray that You will encourage my heart and let my mind settle on the truth. You stand before me and behind me (Ps. 139:1–4), and You will listen to my cries for help (Ps. 116:1). I pray You will help me to see those around me as people I can help. Bring to mind those who need Your help today. Give them grace, peace, and wisdom. I pray for those in the path of Your holy perfect wrath. Give them eyes to see their sin and turn toward grace. Thank You, Jesus, for interceding for me day after day. Your mercies truly are new every morning. Amen.

Resting in God's Goodness

When others harm us or speak bad about us, we want to stand up and make things right. We want to post on social media our perspective and make sure everyone knows the truth. Why do you think it is our tendency to complain, distrust, or get prideful when others treat us poorly?

_____

_____

_____

Christ understands even when others do not. Read Hebrews 3:1–6. How does understanding Christ's intercession for you change the way you think about your life? How is this a comfort?

_____

_____

_____

Praying for others shifts our focus. We are not the only ones suffering hard things. List some people in your life who are going through a hard time. How can you pray for them, based on Moses's prayers for the people?

_____

_____

_____

12

Stepping into an Unknown Future

When I moved to Honduras, I said goodbye to a predictable future. Before we said yes to mission work, our little brick house was to be our home until we were old. I envisioned parties, milestones, and empty rooms as the children slowly left over the years. I looked forward to reading my Bible in the sunroom and hosting friends for Thursday night Bible study. In West Virginia, we had roots which ran decades deep. Our friends and family surrounded us on a daily basis. My family's life wasn't perfect, but it was predictable. In that predictability I took comfort.

God stirred in our hearts to leave predictability because the gospel is everything, eternity is coming, and souls matter. In my mind I knew walking away from our life in the States would mean I would walk away from security, but I didn't grasp the depths of how much we would give up.

My heart worries, doubts, and frets because I want a solid future. I want to prepare and make plans. God, instead, is teaching me foundation cannot be found in my plans or ability to understand the future. Several times in my life God has pulled the rug out from under me and my plans. When this happens, I'm reminded that the future is in His hands and sometimes trusting Him in the dark way ahead is hard.

Maybe you picked up this book because you've whispered these words to yourself or said them aloud for all to hear:

I didn't sign up for this.

Your life has had plot twists over the years, and you just want to know what to expect. I'm sorry I can't tell you what your future looks like, but I can tell you Who holds your future. You might want a handbook for next steps or the secret to discovering God's plan for your life. Even in the midst of all of the messiness that is my life, I've learned a few valuable lessons. The main truth is this: God is so incredibly good. At first I struggled to see how He could be good, but He is. You can believe this too. Moses shows us how.

My husband and I had envisioned our lives retiring in Honduras, but God changed that plan. At the time, when it happened, there was no Plan B for us. The way it was handled felt hurtful, and we struggled those first six months to find our footing. We questioned whether God would ever use us again as missionaries. The future, even today, is still unclear. We have short-term plans, but as far as retirement, I have no idea where we will be in ten or twenty years.

Maybe today you were walking through life and suddenly a fog has settled on the path before you.

What is my next step?

Where do I go from here?

How will this turn out?

Maybe Moses asked those questions as well. The people of Israel were headed to the Promised Land, but even though they knew that, the future was still uncertain. Moses was not going to lead them into the land. Moses was at the end of his life. The first thing Moses did for the people in the end was to remind them of where their true home would be. Before we move forward, let's learn how to have a home right now.

A Home for the Homeless

Lord, You have been our dwelling place in all generations. (Ps. 90:1)

More than anything I want a place to feel secure. I want to know I am safe, secure, and at peace. I want a place that feels like home. Home means I am fully known and fully accepted.

In Honduras, I wasn't fully understood. My words would get mixed up in Spanish and my American friends struggled to understand what I was going through. Moving back didn't instantly put me back in the place I had left. The two and half years we lived overseas had changed me. The hurt we experienced returning had shifted my heart in ways I'm still unpacking. More than anything I want to feel like I belong. You do too, don't you?

Moses was a man who had no home and never belonged. For forty years he walked the halls of the palace, but that was not home. Far from Egypt Moses found a place to live among strangers. This would not feel like home either. Miracle after miracle led Moses to the edge of the Promised Land to only have the people rebel. So, the desert was his home, again. Wandering for forty years Moses spoke to the people and talked to God in order to learn His ways. In the end, Moses never entered Canaan.

> "Because you trespassed against Me among the children of Israel at the waters of Meribah Kadesh, in the Wilderness of Zin, because you did not hallow Me in the midst of the children of Israel. Yet you shall see the land before you, though you shall not go there, into the land which I am giving to the children of Israel." (Deut. 32:51–52)

Even in this, God granted Moses mercy. In Deuteronomy 34:4 it says, "Then the LORD said to him, 'This is the land of which I swore to give Abraham, Isaac, and Jacob, saying, "I will give it to your descendants." I have caused you to see it with your eyes, but you shall not cross over there.'" God showed Moses the land.

At the end of Moses's life he knew he would never be able to dwell in the Promised Land, but that land was never the true dwelling place either. For Moses, we know that he died in peace because of Psalm 90. It says in Psalm 90:1, "Lord, You have been our dwelling place in all generations." How did Moses find a place to belong and to feel the satisfaction of life, even with the heartache of not going into the Promised Land?

We want to belong to a place, but what if we belonged to a Person instead?

You and I, sojourners in this life that always feels uncertain, can find a place to belong. Our journey might be filled with twists and turns, but God doesn't leave us without a home. God gives us a home that travels with us. Let's take a look at Psalm 90 to show us what this true home looks like.

In Moses's song and prayer we are going to see God's purpose for our lives. Even if our circumstances never change, and the path before us remains hazy, God has a plan and He can be trusted. If we truly believe God is sovereign and good, we can learn how to daily rest in Him. This truth anchored Moses's life and it can anchor our lives as well. God is both good and sovereign. God walks with us, leading and guiding and preparing the way. But in all of these things, the good and the bad, His heart is always good toward us.

At the end of Moses's life, he was known as the man who belonged to God. God had revealed Himself to Moses. The Lord, Yahweh, God's personal name entered our world in both time and space to be with us. God's very essence is our "dwelling" place. This word can mean tabernacle. God was Moses's tabernacle. God tabernacled with Moses. The Hebrew word also means "habitation." It means home. God is our home.

Just because Moses found a home in God does that mean we can? We might argue that Moses saw the actual glory of God rest upon the tabernacle. Friends, we have the actual glory of God living inside of us as the Holy Spirit indwells each believer. You might feel as if God doesn't speak to you, but the Bible you hold in your hands tells you exactly what God wants you to know. The one that sits on the nightstand beside your bed or on your kitchen table is the actual words of God. Those words teach us, comfort us, and reveal to us God's very heart for us.

Remember Not to Forget

"Only take heed to yourself, and diligently keep yourself, lest you forget the things your eyes have seen and lest they depart from your heart all the days of your life." (Deut. 4:9)

Our home is found in God, but there is something else Moses does for the people. In the book of Deuteronomy Moses recorded what he really wanted to impart to the people. Moses repeats the phrases "remember" and "lest you forget" all throughout the book.

Today, you and I face the seemingly impossible task of walking forward into an unknown future. We don't know what is around the next bend. There are questions.

> Will the Lord cast off forever?
> And will He be favorable no more?
> Has His mercy ceased forever?
> Has His promise failed forevermore?
> Has God forgotten to be gracious?
> Has He in anger shut up His tender mercies?
> (Ps. 77:7–9)

Our life might make us feel like God has forgotten all about us. Instead, let's remember.

> And I said, "This is my anguish;
> But I will remember the years of the right hand of
>   the Most High."

> I will remember the works of the LORD;
> Surely I will remember Your wonders of old.
> (Ps. 77:10–11)

Let me remember. I wrote those words in my journal just three weeks after we were told we had to leave Honduras. My heart was grieving, hurting, and in anguish, as Psalm 77:10 says. Instead of giving in to the bitterness, anger, and pain, I shifted my heart to remember truth about God.

You and I don't have to stay in our questions, worries, or disappointment. But moving forward might involve looking back. What can you remember about God? How has He worked in your own life previously? Where did God show up for you in the past?

I'll admit I had a hard time writing down things to remember about God. At the time of the hurt, all I could recall were times when I felt alone, abandoned, unloved, or rejected. Our friend Moses helps us in Deuteronomy. The entire book is a collection of Moses's last words to the people. It says he spoke these words to the people on the fortieth year of their wandering in the desert, right before they entered the Promised Land (Deut. 1:3).

What kinds of things did Moses tell them to remember? He spends several chapters reminding the people of four things. The first was to remember who they were and where they had been.

> "And remember that you were a slave in the land of Egypt, and the LORD your God brought you out from there by a mighty hand and by an outstretched arm." (Deut. 5:15)

The Israelites had lived in bondage as slaves. They toiled, were persecuted, and faced hardships worse than anything you and I can even imagine. They cried out to God and He heard them. Moses warns the people to not forget where they had been (Deut. 9:7; 16:12). Before God came to us, we were just like those Israelite slaves. Unable to rescue ourselves, we lived a life in bondage to sin. Paul, in Romans 6 and Ephesians 2, reminds us that we were once slaves to our sin, unable to do anything about it!

> And you He made alive, who were dead in trespasses and sins, in which you once walked according to the course of this world, according to the prince of the power of the air, the spirit who now works in the sons of disobedience, among whom also we all once conducted ourselves in the lusts of our flesh, fulfilling the desires of the flesh and of the mind, and were by nature children of wrath, just as the others. (Eph. 2:1–3)

Yes, we are made alive, but we were once separated from God (Isa. 59:2; Eph. 2:12). When the Israelites were in Egypt, not only were they slaves, they were separated from God. Egypt became a place associated with ungodliness. Without God, they were lost, alone, and without hope. Moses tells the people to not forget where they came from!

If you are struggling to remember God's truth about your life, start here. Remember where you once were. Apart from God, you had nothing good. "O my soul, you have said to the Lord, 'You are my Lord, My goodness is nothing apart from You'" (Ps. 16:2). God is all the goodness you need. Because of Christ's sacrifice, you have been brought near. Rejoice and give thanks for this amazing truth.

The next thing Moses tells the people to remember is what God did to rescue them. God redeemed them from their pain. God used Moses to speak to Pharaoh, but God was the one doing the signs and wonders. Remember the plagues. Remember the Red Sea. God performed miracle after miracle to reveal His power, provision, and protection over the people. Why? To redeem them.

The idea of redemption weaves throughout the Bible like a thread connecting every story and song. God is not finished redeeming His people. You and I are part of His people whom He has redeemed. Not only do we remember how hopeless we were, but how God swept in with all of the hope to rescue us.

> "You shall remember that you were a slave in the land of Egypt, and the LORD your God redeemed you." (Deut. 15:15)

> He has delivered us from the power of darkness and conveyed us into the kingdom of the Son of His love. (Col. 1:13)

God is still in the business of rescuing. Remember that God has rescued you. If He sent His Son, Jesus Christ, to redeem your soul for heaven, how much more does He care for the smallest of hurts in your heart? Can you and I believe He will redeem even this season of disruption?

I believe He is already redeeming it; we need only believe and trust. As our family relocated back to the United States, my heart did not understand how God was working. Looking at where we are now, I can already see God's redemption. I see His protection and His love for us. It takes faith to believe God is sovereign and good even here. While we searched for housing, we lived with my parents. During that time my heart clung to the truth that God was still redeeming—even this.

The next thing Moses reminds the people is that God led them in the wilderness.

> "And you shall remember that the LORD your God led you all the way these forty years in the wilderness." (Deut. 8:2)

For forty years God did not allow their shoes to wear out nor did their clothes get old. Each day He provided manna to eat and water to drink. The Bible says in Deuteronomy 2:7, "For the LORD your God has blessed you in all the work of your hand. He knows your trudging through this great wilderness. These forty years the Lord your God has been with you; you have lacked nothing."

They lacked nothing. You and I might go through times when life feels empty, lonely, and barren, but we will lack nothing. While we had to leave almost all of our possessions in Honduras, we had enough. While we did not have a house of our own for four months, God gave us a place with my mom and dad. Each time a financial need came up, God moved and provided. Each time my heart struggled to trust, God would speak through a message, a sermon, or a song to give me the hope for just one more day.

God will provide what we need.

> And my God shall supply all your needs according to His riches in glory by Christ Jesus. (Phil. 4:19)

If you lack it, then you don't need it right now. That is a hard pill to swallow, but it is true when we take an honest look at our lives. God will give you what you need. Remember all of the times He has provided just what you need. Don't forget His provision!

Finally, Moses spends the majority of the book of Deuteronomy telling the people to remember the commandments and covenant of the Lord. Deuteronomy 1:5 says, "Moses began to explain this law . . ." Moses talks about the laws, the commands, and the promises God gave to the people.

> "Take heed to yourselves, lest you forget the covenant of the LORD your God which He made with you." (Deut. 4:23)

Not only were the people instructed to remember to obey, they were to remember the covenant—*why* they should obey. A covenant is a promise made by two people. God entered into an agreement with the children of Israel.

Moses repeats these commands: Love God, serve Him. Why? Because God chose them and loved them. Even in their sinful state, God extended mercy. Isn't that what God does for us as well? God has chosen us because of His great love for us. Even in our sin He extends mercy. In response to God's great love, we will want to seek and serve Him.

> He has shown you, O man, what is good;
> And what does the LORD require of you
> But to do justly,
> To love mercy,
> And to walk humbly with your God?
> (Micah 6:8)

God has shown us how to move forward. Yes. We can remember, but we can also serve and love God. What is the greatest commandment? Jesus speaks about this in Matthew 22:34–40. In this New Testament passage Jesus quotes Deuteronomy 6:4–5, "Hear, O Israel: The LORD our God, the LORD is one! You shall love the LORD your God with all your heart, with all your soul, and with all your strength."

Serve and love God with your heart. Why? Because in serving and loving God we remember! We remember all God has done, does, and will continue to do for us. We can have confidence, rest, peace, joy, and contentment.

In Psalm 77 the psalmist is in anguish, but then the turning point is when he remembers.

> And I said, "This is my anguish;
> But I will remember the years of the right hand of
>   the Most High."
> I will remember the works of the LORD;
> Surely, I will remember Your wonders of old.
> I will also meditate on all Your work,
> And talk of Your deeds.
> (Ps. 77:10–12)

What does the author of this psalm remember? He remembers the ten plagues (Ps. 77:14–15), the waters of the Red Sea (Ps. 77:16), the pillar of cloud of protection (Ps. 77:17), the mountain of God Psalm 77:18–19), and God's leading "like a flock" (Ps. 77:20).

Remember today all God has done to rescue, redeem, lead, and provide for you. I've seen God's faithful hand draw me near when my heart was overwhelmed with bringing home a daughter with special needs. God provided for everything we needed when we were adopting but also during the pandemic. When the water truck came on the same day we needed water, it reminds me of His promise to provide for our needs. God has rescued me from the bondage of sin and shame. Let me not forget the power of the cross to redeem my life.

You could write a book on all of the times God has been faithful to you. Maybe today you can start with just a page. Use the page at the end of this book and begin writing down all of the things God is calling you to remember. Remembering and recording can be a powerful tool in moving forward.

Moses spends the entire book of Deuteronomy reminding the people of how God was near to them (Deut. 4:7), had provided for them (Deut. 2:7), and rescued them (Deut. 8:2–5). God has done the same for me and you. Don't forget to remember. Look back and see how God has met all of your needs and has drawn close to you.

Out of nowhere something happens, and the life you and I had planned suddenly looks quite different. We are left with uncertainty, disappointment, even heartbreak. In these moments I am tempted to question everything: my purpose, the choices that led me here, even my faith. Have you questioned your faith during this season? It is okay if you have.

Yes, we want to grow through the hurt and disappointment—but we don't know how. There is more to just enduring this season. You and I want to see purpose in it. You want to know that God hasn't left you and that He has good things waiting for you.

A life filled with unexpected twists and turns doesn't have to be a wasted life. Instead, it holds the potential to reveal God's plan, presence, promises, and purpose. We have seen with Moses that even in unforeseen circumstances, we can proclaim God's sovereign goodness. God does not leave us without purpose. In Psalm 90:17 Moses writes, "Yes, establish the work of our hands." God has work for you and me to do.

As we packed up the surgical center, only serving there two years, our hearts broke into a million pieces. We were leaving a work we loved. My husband barely scratched the surface of the potential for that place. God has now called us to do a different work. We don't know what that work looks like. We don't know where that work will lead us. To another country? To another state? Right around the corner? We just don't know yet.

Stepping into the future with hope means we have found a home in God. It also means we look back and remember all God has done for us. Our story isn't over, but by looking at Moses's story we can take comfort in knowing that ultimately the story isn't about us. Record where God has you today. Then look back to where He has already led you. In remembering we can take a step forward. Because when we step into the unknown future, we are stepping hand in hand with a God who is known and has secured our future with Him.

One night several months ago I spoke to my husband about growing roots. I was tired of living in the in-between. We told God that we would settle in Honduras until He moved us. We didn't know that He was preparing during that time for us to move again. Turns out, our roots weren't going to run deep in Honduras. We were growing roots there in Central America only to have to dig up everything again. I want to have a solid plan and to know where God will lead. But God doesn't work that way. God is asking me to keep walking by faith. Instead of trying to grow roots in a place, a relationship, or a job, I'm learning to grow roots in God.

After reading Moses's story and reflecting on your own story, the circumstances of your life might look exactly the same as it did when you started reading. Just reading a book won't change your life, but it can change the way you look at your life. Would you like to sing with Moses right now, *Lord, You have been our dwelling place in all generations?* Moses was at the end of his life when he penned those words. You don't have to wait until the end of your story to see the beauty in a shifting plan. Find your home in God today.

You don't have to wait until life gets back on track before you start living with intentionality, confidence, and purpose. We have the advantage of seeing the end of Moses's life. But you and I don't have that privilege for our own endings. Right now you are still living your story each day.

Romans 8:28 says, "And we know that all things work together for good to those who love God, to those who are the called according to His purpose."

You and I know God is actively working to make our life good, even right now. You are called and loved by God. It doesn't seem fair sometimes that we have to walk through uncertainty in this life. God reminds us, even in this, He is still good.

God is still sovereign and He is still good. Even now I have to ask myself, do I really believe this truth? The circumstances definitely don't feel good. My life feels out of control right now. I'm not sure how this will turn out to be good. The path is still uncertain. We have a lot of things we don't understand, but we can know for sure that God has always been faithful.

Looking back at my life I can tell you: God is good and He is sovereign. Not because everything has turned out great. It hasn't. But my story isn't over. I'm in the messy middle of a story that continues to shift. You are still in the middle of your story too. Moses's story might be over, but ours is still being written. Trusting God's purpose means we can grow spiritually; and this truth is never thwarted or wasted by choices or circumstances.

Believe in God's sovereign goodness. It has the ability to give you peace right now. God wasn't just good in the past, nor is His goodness reserved for the future. Good things are not just around the corner, as most Christian cliches would like you to believe. God is already good, right now. Today. God is working—actively and in the present-tense—everything for your good.

In God's goodness we can see His sovereignty over our lives, even the unforeseen (by us) circumstances. Your life is ordained by a good God; not a vengeful, merciless, or absent God. This goodness is found because our God is one who provides a purpose for the grief; His comforting presence and rock-solid promises hold tight in the dark nights of heartache. Moving forward, you and I don't have to fear the future or live in the past. We can start today remembering truth.

True rest and true peace are possible.

The daily practices of prayer and Bible reading shift my heart back. It can do the same for you. Let's begin to remind our hearts back to the sovereign goodness of God.

God was not the one who hurt us. Yes, He allowed the hurt to enter. May we remember that even with the suffering, God's good and sovereign plan means His intent was not evil. His intent for us is never evil and only good.

> You will keep him in perfect peace,
> Whose mind is stayed on You,
> Because he trusts in You.
> (Isa. 26:3)

You will indeed, God, keep me in perfect peace when my mind is stayed on You. Amen.

Remember and Record

_____

_____

_____

_____

_____

_____

_____

_____

_____

_____

_____

_____

_____

_____

_____

_____

_____

_____

Notes

1. Matthew Henry's Commentary on Exodus 2:1–4, https://www.biblegateway.com/resources/matthew-henry/Exod.2.1–Exod.2.4.

2. J. M. Boice, *The Life of Moses: God's First Deliverer of Israel* (Blackstone Audio, 2018), audiobook.

3. Andrew Murray, *True Vine* (Moody Classics) (Chicago, IL: Moody Publishers, 2007).

4. Oswald Chambers, *My Utmost for His Highest* (1935; repr., Grand Rapids: Discovery House, 1992), October 21 devotional.

5. Warren W. Wiersbe, *Be Delivered: Finding Freedom by Following God* (Old Testament Commentary Exodus) (Colorado Springs: David C. Cook: 2010), 23.

6. F. B. Meyer, *Devotional Commentary on Exodus* (Grand Rapids: Kregel Publishers, 1978).

7. Edward T. Welch, *Depression: Looking Up from the Stubborn Darkness* (Greensboro, NC: New Growth Press, 2011), 31.

8. Definition for *intercede* can be found at dictionary.com.

9. Matthew George Easton, "Intercession of Christ," *Easton Bible Dictionary* (New York: Scriptura Press, 2015), https://www.biblestudytools.com/dictionaries/eastons-bible-dictionary/inter-cession-of-christ.html.